Uncle Jo

Facts to

ANNOY

Your Teacher

S.S. UNCLE

U.J. SCHOOL

TEACHER

Duh!

BATHROOM READER FOR KIDS ONLY

By the Bathroom Readers' Institute

OUR REGULAR READERS RAVE

Some books print fancy reviews written by critics. Not us! Here at the BRI, we care more about what our faithful readers have to say.

"I got the *Book of Fun* when I was 9 and I am 11 now, and I still can't put it down. I am always the class clown in school and I would be way boring without your book."

—**Nick**

"Your books are awesome, both me and my brother love them. Go with the flow and never quit!"

—**Rubaiyat**

"The information in your books fascinates me and is so interesting. For Christmas, half of my list is Bathroom Reader books. The coolest things about your books is that all of the facts are so funny."

—**Sabrina**

"Hello BRI! You guys rock. I'm a huge fan, and I read your books everyday...my Social Studies teacher thinks I'm never paying attention."

—**Jonathan**

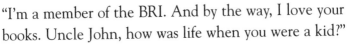

"I'm a member of the BRI. And by the way, I love your books. Uncle John, how was life when you were a kid?"

—**Ryan**

"I love your books so much! I was about 8 or 9 when I got my first Bathroom Reader. It was called *Uncle John's Book of Fun*. Now I'm 11 and have 6 of your books. My goal is to have all of your books. Keep up the good work, and as you always say.... go with the flow!

—**Aaron**

"I love Uncle John's *Wild & Woolly Bathroom Reader* book. It was so funny and I learned a lot of fact about animals! Thank-you Uncle John, and keep writing the good books!"

—**Sarah**

"I love the Bathroom Readers. They give me random trivia for class and help me look smart."

—**Dylan**

"Hi, my name is Steven. I've read *Top Secret Bathroom Reader*, *Book of Fun*, the first *Kids Only*, and love them all! I can't wait until the next one. Thank you Uncle John, Porter, and everyone else in the Bathroom Readers' Institute for making my life so much better!"

—**Steven**

Uncle John's®

Facts to
ANNOY
Your Teacher

BATHROOM
READER
FOR
KIDS
ONLY!

By the Bathroom Readers' Institute

Ashland, Oregon, and San Diego, California

UNCLE JOHN'S
FACTS TO ANNOY YOUR TEACHER
BATHROOM READER FOR KIDS ONLY

"Bathroom Reader," "Portable Press," and
"Bathroom Readers' Institute" are registered trademarks
of Baker & Taylor, Inc. All rights reserved.

For information, write...
The Bathroom Readers' Institute
P.O. Box 1117, Ashland, OR 97520
www.bathroomreader.com
e-mail: mail@bathroomreader.com

ISBN-13: 978-1-59223-982-5 / ISBN-10: 1-59223-982-X

Library of Congress Cataloging-in-Publication Data
Uncle John's bathroom reader for kids only : facts to annoy your
teacher.
p. cm.
ISBN 978-1-59223-982-5 (pbk.)
1. Curiosities and wonders--Juvenile literature. 2. Children's
questions and answers. 3. American wit and humor. I. Bathroom
Readers' Institute (Ashland, Or.)
AG195.U526 2009
031.02--dc22
2009007508

Printed in the United States of America
09 10 11 12 13 14 15   8 7 6 5 4 3 2 1

THANK YOU!

The Bathroom Readers' Institute thanks the following people whose help made this book possible.

Gordon Javna
JoAnn Padgett
Melinda Allman
Andy Peterson
Brian Boone
Dan Mansfield
Jeff Altemus
Amy Miller
Jay Newman
Michael Brunsfeld
Julia Papps
Myles Callum
Vickey Kalambakal
Cathy Hall
Debbie Pawlak
Katherine Butler
Katy Duffield
Leslie Elman
Rose Kivi
Liana Mahoney
Jenny Burr

Louise Peacock
J. Carroll
Jennifer Mercer
Peggy Deland
Malcolm Hillgartner
Terry Miller Shannon
Kathryn Grogman
Suzanne Francis
William I. Lengeman
Amy L. and Lisa M.
Monica Maestas
Sydney Stanley
David Cully
Ginger Winters
Jennifer Frederick
David Calder
Karen Malchow
Erin Corbin
R. R. Donnelley
Sophie and Bea
Porter the Wonder Dog

TABLE OF CONTENTS

Because the BRI understands your reading needs, we've divided the contents by length as well as subject:

Short: A quick read

Medium: 2 pages

Long: 3 to 4 pages (That's not too long, is it?)

*   *   *

SCHOOL DAZE

"Thank goodness I was never sent to school; it would have rubbed off some of the originality."

—Beatrix Potter, author

"The difference between school and life? In school, you're taught a lesson and then given a test. In life, you're given a test that teaches you a lesson."

—Tom Bodett, author

"School's a weird thing. I'm not sure it works."

—Johnny Depp

GREETINGS FROM UNCLE JOHN

PSST!
This book is your secret weapon. You see, adults like to pretend that they know all the answers. But we know they don't really. For example, ask your teacher or your dad or your friend's mom (or your friend's teacher's mom) why people drive on a parkway but park in a driveway. They'll probably look confused and blurt out, "Because that's the way it is!" But after reading *Uncle John's Facts to Annoy Your Teacher*, you'll be able to tell them why. (And if they get annoyed by being outsmarted by a kid, that's a bonus!)

This book is yours. Do whatever you want with it. Draw cartoons in the corners of the pages, mark up the puzzles, color in the pictures. And all the while, you'll absorb the fascinating information we've gathered for you. How can we be so sure? We've been making *Bathroom Readers* for kids for a long time, and they've all passed the "it doesn't suck" test. Here's just some of what's inside:

- **You want gross? We've got gross.** The man who "sang" with farts, booger-licking bison, sweaty facts, and a trip to the vomitorium. (Yuck!)

- **Rebellious kids.** The girls whose tale of real fairies

baffled grown-ups, the future president who got sent to the principal's office, and a nine-year-old professional guitar player. Oh, and a kid who squirts milk out of his eyes.

- **Surefire ways to annoy people.** Learn to speak hobo, make a bloody eyeball, build a better spitball, and play your armpits.
- **History that isn't boring.** An escape from Alcatraz, the guy who invented Mr. Potato Head, the origin of the doughnut, and pirate treasure that's still waiting to be found.

But be warned: After you read this book, you'll be smarter than most of the people around you. And as Spider-Man's uncle once said, "With great power comes great responsibility." (Or was that what Porter the Wonder Dog told me when he sent me to the store for his favorite dog biscuits?) Anyway, it's your solemn duty to annoy those around you with your newfound wisdom. Speak to them gently, since their brains may not be able to comprehend facts of this magnitude.

Now it's time to dive into the most fun and fact-filled books in the history of books! (Okay, maybe *one* of the most.) Happy reading. And as always, Go with the Flow!

**—Uncle John, the BRI Staff, and
Porter the Wonder Dog**

WRONG FACTS

Teachers say a lot of things.
Not all of them are true.

FACT? *Cinco de Mayo (May 5) is Mexico's version of the Fourth of July.*
WRONG! Cinco de Mayo is more widely celebrated in the United States than in Mexico, where it's pretty much confined to the south-central state of Puebla. Not only is it not a major holiday, it's not even Mexico's independence day. Cinco de Mayo commemorates the 1862 Battle of Puebla, in which the Mexican army fought back an invasion by France. Mexico's actual independence day—celebrating its freedom from Spain—is on September 16.

FACT? *George Washington had wooden teeth.*
WRONG! In 2005, the National Museum of Dentistry performed tests on four sets of dentures known and proven to have been used by the first president of the United States. The findings: The false teeth contained a variety of materials...but no wood. Washington's various chompers were made out of combinations of gold, horse teeth, donkey teeth, hippopotamus tusks, and even human teeth. They were held together with metal springs, screws, and bolts.

Flamingos build their nests with mouthfuls of mud.

WISE GUYS

Cool advice from some cool guys.

"In order to succeed, your desire for success should be greater than your fear of failure."
—**Bill Cosby**

"All you need is love. But a little chocolate now and then doesn't hurt."
—**Charles M. Schulz**

"I don't know what my calling is, but I want to be here for a bigger reason. I strive to be like the greatest people who have ever lived.."
—**Will Smith**

"Fishing is boring, unless you catch an actual fish, and then it is disgusting."
—**Dave Barry**

"Nothing to me feels as good as laughing incredibly hard."
—**Steve Carell**

"The three little sentences that will get you through life. Number 1: Cover for me. Number 2: Oh, good idea, Boss! Number 3: It was like that when I got here."
—**Homer Simpson**

"You get ideas from daydreaming. You get ideas from being bored. You get ideas all the time."
—**Neil Gaiman**

Always do right. This will gratify some people and astonish the rest.
—**Mark Twain**

FREAKY FOOD

You won't find fried tarantulas in your cafeteria—unless you live in Cambodia. Some people have all the luck!

PICKLED BEET BURGERS

Welcome to Australia—home of kangaroos, dingoes, and...beetroot burgers? Beets, which Australians call "beetroot," are as common a condiment on burgers Down Under as lettuce and tomato are in the United States. According to beetroot-burger lovers, a slice of the cooked or pickled veggie adds "extra juiciness and an earthy flavor." Folks who are anti-beet, of course, mention the fact that beets "taste like dirt" as the number-one reason not to include them. The number-two reason? Try getting a beet-juice stain out of your clothes. (A special treat: burgers in Sydney, Australia, often come with beets...and a fried egg.)

FRIED TARANTULAS

Among the best-known delicacies in Cambodia are *a-ping*, or fried tarantulas. And the town that's made a name for itself by producing the best quality

a-ping is Skun, about 46 miles northeast of the country's capital, Phnom Penh. Tourists and Cambodians flock to Skun every summer when the tarantulas are in season. (The fattest and most plentiful are found in the forest near the town.) Be sure to eat them like the locals: fried to kill the spider's venom and then dipped in a mixture of garlic and salt. According to some Cambodians, fried tarantulas are tastier than American fast food.

ROASTED ANTS

If you went to a movie theater in Colombia and wanted to fit in, you wouldn't order popcorn. You'd ask for this traditional Colombian snack: a paper cone filled with roasted ants. One tourist said that they are "delicious when salted."

*   *   *

THIS MIGHT MAKE YOU GAG

Throwing up after a big meal was considered to be a status symbol in ancient Rome because it showed off your wealth. If you ate so much that you made yourself sick, you were clearly better off than the lower classes, who hardly had enough money to buy food at all. (Even Julius Caesar liked to vomit after a big dinner.) But contrary to popular belief, the Romans didn't vomit in *vomitoriums*. Why? A vomitorium was actually a passageway in a theater or sports arena that people would "spew out of" when the play or event was over.

BANNED BOOKS

Why would anybody discourage reading?

Alice's Adventures in Wonderland, by Lewis Carroll
In 1931, the Chinese government banned this book because it gave animals human emotions and characteristics. "Animals," one government official said, "should not use human language."

Blubber, by Judy Blume
This children's novel tells the story of a girl who participates in the constant torment of a classmate, only to learn a valuable lesson when she becomes the object of the teasing herself. In 1990, a parent in Louisville, Kentucky, asked that it be removed from her child's elementary school because the characters "behaved unkindly" (which is the whole point of the book).

A Light in the Attic, by Shel Silverstein
Cunningham Elementary School in Beloit, Wisconsin, took this humorous poetry collection off its library shelves in 1985 because one poem jokingly encouraged kids to break dishes instead of washing them.

Little Red Riding Hood, by the Brothers Grimm
Was the Big Bad Wolf eating people too violent? Nope. Officials in two California school districts thought the story might encourage kids to drink because one of the illustrations shows a bottle of wine among the food Red brings to her grandmother.

Where's Waldo?, by Martin Handford
The public libraries of Saginaw, Michigan, tried to ban the first Waldo book in 1989 because some of the pages supposedly contained "dirty things"—like the bare back of a sunbather in a beach scene.

Mickey Mouse comics
In 1938, just before World War II, Italy's National Conference of Juvenile Literature banned all books featuring Mickey Mouse. Why? The organization thought the character encouraged kids to think for themselves and be individuals, concepts that clashed with the politics of Italy's dictator at the time, Benito Mussolini.

The Diary of a Young Girl, by Anne Frank
Anne Frank's diary is a sad account of her time living in an attic and hiding from the Nazis during World War II. In 1983, the Alabama Textbook Commission tried to remove the book from schools because the group thought it was "a real downer."

BIZARRE ANIMAL ACTS

Some critters do people tricks better than people.

MONKEYING AROUND

Macaque monkeys often imitate human beings, but none do it better than Momoko, a monkey who lives in Nagasaki, Japan. She scuba dives, water-skis, windsurfs, and snow skis.

Her owner, Katsumi Nakashima, adopted Momoko from a shelter. He got her used to the water in his bathtub and then took her boating. At first, he towed the monkey slowly behind his boat on a four-foot-long surfboard with handlebars. But soon Momoko was shooting across the water on water skis at almost 20 mph.

The six-year-old monkey's favorite sport, however, is scuba diving. Wearing a yellow wetsuit and a breathing mask made to fit her face, Momoko swims to the ocean floor on her own and sits on a rock watching the colorful fish swim by.

PIG OUT

There's a saying: "Don't try to teach a pig to sing," meaning don't attempt the impossible. But teach a pig to ride a skateboard, play songs, and golf? That's not so hard...at least not for Bacon and Porkchop, two potbel-

---

lied pigs from Colorado. The pair can do dozens of incredible tricks, like shooting a ball through a basketball hoop and raising a flag.

It all started in the 1990s when Lynne Vincent convinced her husband John to bring home a little black piglet named Bacon from an animal shelter. Pigs have a good memory, which makes them fast learners. "I just started training him to be smarter than my friends' dogs," John recalled. It worked. After a few weeks of training, Bacon had learned all the typical commands: he could shake, turn in a circle, and fetch. From there, it wasn't a big leap to 360-degree slam dunks and jumping 18-inch hurdles.

Bacon was later paired with another pig that Lynne and John adopted, a white piglet named Porkchop. The two became a stage team. They sing and act (and learned to do impersonations of James Bond, Stevie Wonder, and Elvis Presley). Porkchop even landed a role on an episode of the television show *Diagnosis: Murder*. And when the pair performed on *The Tonight Show*, Jay Leno observed, "Pigs like this only come around once in a lifetime."

British astronomer William Whewell coined the term "scientist" in 1833.

TOENAILS

You've got 10 toenails—so how about 10 toenail facts?

1. MOON SPOTS

That white spot at the base of your toenails (and finger-nails) shaped like a half-moon is called the "lunule," a name that comes from the Latin word for "moon."

2. WORLD'S LONGEST

In 1991, a woman from California named Louise Hollis set (and still holds) the record for the longest combined toenail length: her 10 nails were 7.25 feet long. How much time does she spend filing and painting them? Two days every week.

3. CLIP ME TENDER

The Loudermilk Boarding House Museum in Georgia contains about 30,000 Elvis Presley artifacts. Here you'll find a wart, a vial of sweat, and a toe-nail...all said to have come

from the King himself. (Some Elvis experts debate the authenticity of the toenail, though, so it's just called the "Maybe Elvis Toenail.")

4. OUCH!

About 5 percent of people complain of ingrown toenails, that painful condition where the toenail grows into the surrounding skin.

5. ANOTHER KIND OF TOENAIL

The Devil's Toenail in Llano County, Texas, is a 350-foot-tall sandstone hill that looks like a giant toenail.

6. MOTHER KNOWS BEST

Gorilla mothers use their teeth to trim their babies' toenails.

7. TOENAILS TELL THE TALE

The chemicals in your toenails can tell doctors lots of things: if you're at risk for skin cancer or heart disease, what you eat and drink, whether you take prescription drugs, and even where you've lived.

8. A STAR IS BORN

Thomas John Ashton's 1852 book *A Treatise on Corns,*

Bunions, and Ingrowing of the Toenail: Their Cause and Treatment contains a section on toenails. It's believed to have been the first time the subject of toenails showed up in a published book.

9. FAST HANDS
Toenails grow four times more slowly than fingernails. (It takes about eight months to grow a new toenail.)

10. NECKNAILS
Marathon runner Jan Ryerse was always breaking off parts of his toenails when he ran races. (They collected in his shoes.) So he decided to craft a memento: a toenail necklace. Most of the toenails are his, but he also took donations from family, friends, and fans to fill it out.

*   *   *

TAKE HEART
- People who've suffered a bad breakup or the death of a loved one are more likely to have a heart attack.
- Most people think their heart is located on the left side of their chest, but it's not. Your heart is in the center, right between your lungs.
- Make a fist—your heart is about that size.

GOSSIP!

Stuff you didn't know about celebrities.

- Both of **Jack Black's** parents were rocket scientists.

- When he was a young man, **President Richard Nixon** worked at an Arizona carnival. As a young man, **President Gerald Ford** was a model.

- **Rihanna's** real name: Robyn Fenty.

- **Ashton Kutcher, Jon Heder** (*Napoleon Dynamite*), and **Scarlett Johansson** all have twin siblings.

- **Cameron Diaz** washes her face only with bottled Evian water.

- **Kelly Clarkson** initially wanted to be a marine biologist. Then she saw the shark movie *Jaws*, changed her mind, and decided to be a singer instead.

- **Barack Obama** met his wife Michelle when he took a job at a law firm in Chicago—she was his boss.

- When she was 11, singer **Taylor Swift** won a national poetry contest. Her entry: a three-page poem called "Monster in My Closet."

- Right before he was supposed to record his first album in 2003, **Kanye West** was in a car accident, which required his jaw to be wired shut. He didn't quit rapping, though. Instead, he sneaked out of the hospital and recorded his first single, "Through the Wire"— with his jaw still wired shut.

If Oprah Winfrey married writer Deepak Chopra, she'd be Oprah Chopra.

CIRCUS SUPERSTITIONS

*When Uncle John was a teenager, he ran off to join
the circus…as a toilet paper roll juggler, of course.
So to honor his fellow performers (and lucky
page #13), he put together this list.*

- **Don't sleep inside the big top.** It could collapse, and anyone inside might be killed.

- **Never look back during a parade.** Circus performers always keep their eyes forward to leave behind any misfortune or bad memories.

- **Don't whistle under the big top.** Before high-tech headsets and computers, the backstage workers at a circus whistled to each other to give stage cues: when to drop a curtain, when to light the human cannon, etc. If the performers whistled, too, it could throw off the entire show. Today, no one whistles…just in case.

- **Don't count the audience.** This old theater superstition applies to the circus as well and was designed to protect the performers. If the audience was too small, it might make them feel self-conscious; too large, and they might get stage fright.

- **Never take a picture of an elephant's trunk pointing down**—it will make the circus's luck run out.

THE FART MAN

*Forget what your teachers may have told you—some
jobs require skills you can't learn in school.*

T HAR SHE BLOWS!
Joseph Pujol was born in France in 1857, and
as a teenager, he discovered that he had a
unique and special talent: he could fart at will. One
day, while swimming in the ocean, Joseph took a deep
breath before dunking his head underwater. When he
breathed in, he felt a whoosh of cold water enter his
body through his bottom. Soon, Joseph started doing
the trick to entertain his friends: he'd suck in water
through his behind and then shoot it out. Then, he
discovered he could also do it with air.

After high school, Pujol joined the army and honed
his farting skills by performing them for other soldiers.
He learned to make different notes with his farts and
even played tunes on a small flute called an ocarina.

A CHEEKY STAGE ACT

When he left the army, Pujol went to work as a baker
(and earned a reputation for making fantastic muffins).
But in 1887, he wanted a change in life, so he put
together a farting act and landed a gig at the most
famous theater in Paris: the Moulin Rouge.

On the night of his first stage appearance, the audience initially didn't know what to think. He started

off imitating cannon fire and thunder, blowing out can-
dles, and tooting out songs on his ocarina. Finally, the
audience started to laugh...and laugh. Some women
even fainted from all the laughing because their corsets
were so tight they couldn't take deep enough breaths.

THE SWEET SMELL OF SUCCESS

Pujol's act quickly became popular, and within two
years he was the highest-paid entertainer in France.
He kept up his unusual job until he retired in 1914.

When Pujol died in 1945, the famous Sorbonne
University in Paris asked his family to donate his body
to science...so doctors at its medical school could study
his insides and figure out how he was able to make such
incredible farts. But his family turned them down and
instead buried him at a cemetery in southern France.

Actual headline: TREES CAN BREAK WIND.

SP⚽RTS STUPIDITY

Sports stars make great plays, but they can also make some really bad decisions. Like these guys.

- In 1912, a team of college all-stars—the **Norfolk Blues**—challenged the football team at Gallaudet University in Washington, D.C., to a game. The Blues thought they'd have no trouble clobbering their opponent because Gallaudet had a lower-ranked team. So they were shocked when the underdogs shut them out 20–0. How did they win? Gallaudet is a college for the deaf, and the Blues talked openly about what plays they were going to run, thinking they were safe because the Gallaudet players couldn't hear them. The kicker? Gallaudet teaches all of its students to lip-read.

- The Dallas Cowboys were playing the Buffalo Bills in the Super Bowl in 1993 when Cowboys defenseman **Leon Lett** recovered a fumble and headed for his team's end zone. But then he made a stupid mistake. A couple of yards before he crossed the goal line, he started celebrating his "certain" touchdown...and didn't see the Bills' Don Beebe coming up behind him. Beebe stripped the ball, and Lett didn't score.

*　　*　　*

"Always root for the winner. That way, you won't be disappointed."　　**—Tug McGraw, baseball player**

Q: What 7-letter word contains 10 words without rearranging any letters?...

MUSEUMS THAT ARE FUN!

*Everyone loves to get out of class once in a while…okay,
all the time. Next time your teacher asks for
ideas, suggest one of these museums.*

THE COCKROACH HALL OF FAME
There aren't many people who'd set up an
entire museum dedicated to one of the ickiest
insects ever to crawl the earth. But exterminator
Michael Bohdan from Plano, Texas, did. He's always
been fascinated by bugs and, in the 1980s, entered a
contest looking for the biggest cockroach in Texas. His
two-inch-long roach (now mounted behind glass on his
office wall) won first place and the $1,000 prize. And
that got him thinking…what about a museum full of
roaches?

So next door to his pest-control shop, Bohdan
opened the Cockroach Hall of Fame. His main attraction: dead cockroaches dressed up in tiny outfits and
placed in various scenes. There's Marilyn Monroach, a
musician roach playing the piano, two roaches sun-
bathing on a miniature beach, and more than 20 others.
Plus, there's a display of live Madagascar hissing cockroaches, and visitors can hold the bugs…if they have
the courage.

DEAD SQUIRREL-VILLE

In 1995, Sam Sanfillippo was a mortician living in Madison, Wisconsin, when he took up taxidermy as a hobby. (A taxidermist stuffs the skins of dead animals so they can be put on display.) His subjects? Dead squirrels. Sanfillippo says he uses "ones that had been hit by cars or died of heart attacks or whatever." He put them on display in the basement of the Cress Funeral Home, where he worked.

In the years since, Sanfillippo has put together a collection of stuffed, mounted squirrels in various poses. There's a squirrel on a bucking bronco, five squirrels playing poker, a squirrel "family" riding a Ferris wheel, and dozens of others. And it wasn't all just for fun. Sanfillippo says the stuffed squirrels made the people who came to funerals at his mortuary feel more relaxed: "They don't know what to do—the old people—at funerals, you know." So he'd send them into the basement to look at the squirrels, and they'd always come out laughing. Today, the collection is called the Dead Pals of Sam Sanfillippo, and anyone can visit them.

MORE WEIRD MUSEUMS

- Circus World Museum: Baraboo, Wisconsin
- The Museum of Bad Art: Deadham, Massachusetts
- Kansas Barbed Wire Museum: Lacrosse, Kansas
- International UFO Museum and Research Center: Roswell, New Mexico

THE DIRT ON DIRT

*It's everywhere…underfoot, in your clothes,
on your face. What's the deal with dirt?*

- Dirt is made mostly from rocks. Over thousands of years, wind and water erode the rocks into smaller and smaller pieces. Then other things—like animal droppings and dead plants— mix in with the rock dust to create soil.

- About 50 to 250 earthworms make their homes in an average acre of lawn.

- The carpet in your house can hold twice its weight in dirt.

- About 80 percent of the dirt in a house comes inside on people: stuck to their shoes, clothes, skin, and hair.

- People in many cultures (Africa, Mongolia, even the United States) eat mud. They consider it healthy for pregnant women—a way for their bodies to get the minerals they need. One American mud-eater says, "The good stuff is real smooth…just like a piece of candy."

- Some animals, like pigs and elephants, cover themselves in mud to protect and cool their skin.

Found in a fortune cookie: "He who throws dirt loses ground."

DRIVE YOUR TEACHER NUTS

Making trouble in class is an old tradition—students have been doing it for hundreds of years. A few of those time-honored techniques (and some creatures to make your teacher shriek) are hidden in the schoolhouse-shaped puzzle to the right.

ARM FARTING	PRANKS
BUBBLE GUM	PUPPY
BUGS	SALAMANDER
COMIC BOOKS	SILLY NOTES
FAKE EYEBALLS	SNAKES
FERRET	SPIDERS
GARLIC	WHISPERING
ITCHING POWDER	WORMS
NEWT	YO-YO

Say "I love you" in Swahili: *Nakupenda.*

```
                    D
                  C X M
                V O R U B
              D B M E G C X
            C S R I D E T G B
          X C P B C W L K X S B
        S M Y C Q B O B S E L Q E
      Z Z B U G S O P B C I L R A G
    D D G Z O R I O G U U S A E R N H
    C H B     H L K N B P K B D M I M
    V U E     J L S I N A P E N F R T
    F P T O Y O Y M H     Y A A E E
    B R A E H Q N R C     E M R P Z
    G A G D R B O O T     E A T S Q
    P N Z T Y R T W I     K L I I H
    V K S P I D E R S     A A N H M
    M S E K A N S F D     F S G W G
```

Answers on page 242.

Hummingbirds have the highest metabolic rate of any animal on earth.

STAR SECRETS

Uncle John has a talking dog named Porter who can't keep a secret. Last week, he told the mailman all about Uncle John's collection of purple polka-dot underwear. Here are some more secrets that just couldn't stay hidden.

SMARTY PANTS

Actor Matt Damon was such a good student in high school that he was accepted to Harvard University. He attended the college for four years (from 1988 to 1992), but never graduated. He dropped out to become an actor instead.

THE MUSIC MAN

Professional skateboarder Tony Hawk loves to play the violin. He started when he was about six, the same time he got his first skateboard, and played until he was nine. But his two hobbies took up a lot of time, and eventually, he had to make a choice. So he gave up the instrument and concentrated on skateboarding. He always missed playing music, though, so he picked up the violin again as a young adult and has played ever since.

TOP-SECRET INGREDIENT

Cookbook author and television chef Julia Child was doing a lot more than learning to whip up dinner before she became famous. She was a secret agent. During

World War II, Child worked for the Office of Strategic Services (OSS), which was the predecessor of the CIA. One of Child's jobs involved inventing shark repellent; the animals sometimes bumped into under-water explosives and set them off. This let the German submarines know in advance where the bombs were—not so sneaky. So Child and a few other spies got together and made a repellent to coat the bombs and keep the sharks away.

BEFORE THEY WERE FAMOUS

These celebrities also had odd jobs in their younger days:

- Whoopi Goldberg was a bricklayer, funeral makeup artist, and garbage collector.
- Pink cleaned toilets at McDonald's.
- Barack Obama scooped ice cream at Baskin-Robbins.
- Colin Ferrell taught line dancing in Ireland.
- Hugh Jackman worked as a clown. (He didn't have it so bad, though—he often made $50 per hour.)
- Ellen DeGeneres dried cars at a car wash.

WHO AM I?

If teachers really wanted students to look forward to quizzes, they'd ask questions that test our knowledge of important things...like cartoon characters. (Answers are on page 241.)

1. These days, I have a good life in Hawaii (even though swimming was hard for me to learn), but I had to dodge a whole bunch of aliens to stay on earth.

2. Gary kept me up all night with his meowing, and then Patrick told me we couldn't be friends anymore because I was so crabby from lack of sleep that I ate all of his kelp fries. (I'll apologize after a nap.)

3. My dad got fired again today. Mr. Spacely is so rude! But Mom is sure things will be all right again tomorrow. (Psst...Astro says hi.)

4. I have trouble choosing my wishes, but I do my best! It's hard to follow all the instructions in "Da Rules."

5. Hiiiigh-Ya! Fighting Tai Lung made me so hungry that I ate all of the noodles in Dad's cart.

6. We've got a great idea for next summer vacation...if only Candace will keep her big mouth shut!

7. I'm the forgotten middle child, and much smarter than the rest of my family. Only my saxophone keeps me sane.

8. I love to go on adventures, but wish my cousin Angelica would leave me alone.

WELCOME TO WORMTOWN

*This town's squirmy population keeps
a whole lot of people in business.*

THE WORMS CRAWL IN...

Wiscasset, Maine, is known for two things: It's a summer tourist town often called "Maine's prettiest village" because of its historic homes and buildings. It's also famous for its worms.

Wiscasset was originally a shipbuilding town, but in the 1920s, that business started moving to larger cities in the Northeast. That left many people with no jobs. But fortunately, the town had another resource that put people back to work.

THE WORMS CRAWL OUT...

Billions of worms—most notably, fat bloodworms and sandworms—lived in mucky marshes along the coast. At first, residents of Wiscasset considered them to be a nuisance because bloodworms sting and sandworms pinch...painfully.

But by 1930, so many people were out of work and looking for a new way to make money that they began to see the worms differently. Sport fishermen all over New England needed worms for bait, and they'd pay

twice as much per dozen for the juicy worms from
Wiscasset than for skinnier worms from other places.

So men around town pulled on rubber hip boots and
trudged out into the mud to dig up the worms. On a
good day, they could bring in as many as 1,000, and in
1937, the total harvest was about 2.5 million.

GOLD IN THEM THAR WORMS!

Today, men and women in Wiscasset are still in the
worming business. And it's not a bad job. Wormers
work just four or five hours a day. They have to get to
the marshes during low tide, when the water doesn't
cover up the worms. And their season lasts only from
April to October.

The state's worm population has decreased since
the 1930s—because of all the harvesting—but people
can still dig up 300 to 500 worms a day. They generally
make 15 cents for each sandworm and 25 cents per
bloodworm. (The bloodworms are bigger, longer, and
juicier...all the better for
luring fish.) So if you
really like digging
around in muck (and
who doesn't?), then
you too can head
to Maine and
get your
hands
dirty.

OLD RULES

*Ever wonder how your teacher would do in
a 19th-century schoolroom? Here's the way
most teachers lived in the "good old days."*

- In the early 1800s, schoolteachers were almost all
  male. But that changed when school boards realized
  that women were willing to work for less money than
  men. In 1849, the Littleton, Massachusetts, school
  committee wrote: "It seems...very poor policy to pay a
  man $20 or $22 a month for teaching children the
  ABCs, when a female could do the work more successfully at one third of the price."

- Teachers hardly ever had their own homes. Most
  lived with the families of their students. This room
  and board was part of the teacher's pay.

- A teacher's moral character was considered very
  important. An 1872 set of rules from New Hampshire
  said, "Any teacher who smokes, uses liquor in any
  form, [or] frequents pool or public halls...will give
  good reason to suspect his worth, intention, integrity,
  and honesty."

- Female teachers had to remain unmarried. In the
  19th century, the San Francisco Board of Education
  said it would fire "any female teacher who may com-
  mit the crime of marriage."

- Teachers dealt with 19th-century "emergencies," too.

Dr. Seuss's *The Cat in the Hat* contains just 220 words.

Around 1890, a teacher in California described one problem in a letter to her family: "There are many openings in the walls of our school that admit birds, lizards, mice, and snakes. During one lesson, a snake appeared, sticking his tongue out at us. I disposed of him amidst great applause."

- Teachers in the 19th century were allowed to punish their students physically...and they did. An 1860 set of rules for students spelled out the punishments:

Children who are caught writing with their left hand: 1 ruler rap on the knuckles.

Talking in class: 1 whack with a rod.

Chewing tobacco or spitting: 7 whacks.

*   *   *

KEEP YOUR LIPS TO YOURSELF, PLEASE

In February 2009, the Warrington Bank train station in northwest England erected an unfriendly sign: a silhouette of a man and woman puckered up, with a slash through it...no kissing! According to station authorities, the ban was necessary because many commuters took too long kissing their loved ones hello and good-bye—it made the platform crowded. But when word of the ban reached the managers at London's High Wycombe train station, they retaliated with their own sign, proclaiming "Kissing is welcome here! We would never dream of banning kissing!"

FAIRY TALE

About a century ago, two young girls from England walked out of the forest with an amazing story: fairies were real, they said...and they could prove it.

THE CASE OF THE FAIRY PHOTOS

One day in 1917, two cousins—16-year-old Elsie Wright and 10-year-old Frances Griffiths—came home from a walk in the woods. The girls had been playing near a stream on Elsie's parents' property, and Frances had slipped into the water. Her shoes and stockings were wet. Polly Wright, Elsie's mother, was angry when she saw the girls; she'd told them to stay away from the stream. But just as she was about to scold them, Elsie and Frances told an incredible tale: they'd gone to the stream, the girls explained, because they'd met a group of fairies in the woods and had been playing with them. And to prove it, the pair borrowed a camera and rushed back into the forest to take a photo.

GNOME SWEET GNOME

The next day, Elsie's father Arthur developed the picture. In it, Frances posed behind a small mound of dirt while several small creatures that appeared to be fairies danced on branches in front of her. A few months later, the girls went back to the woods and came home with more pictures: Elsie playing with a gnome, a fairy leaping toward Frances, a fairy handing Elsie a flower, and one photo of a group of fairies dancing alone. Arthur developed all the pictures. Despite the girls' insistence that they were real (Elsie even described the gnome's wings as "more mothlike than the fairies'"), he considered them child's play, put them in a drawer, and forgot about them.

MOTHER KNOWS BEST

Elsie's mother, though, didn't forget. Polly Wright was a member of the Theosophist Society, a group that believed in the existence of elves, gnomes, and fairies. At a society meeting two years later, Polly told the group the girls' fairy tale and showed everyone the old photos.

The head of the Theosophist Society was a man named Edward Gardner. After examining the photos, he declared them real and...people just believed him. Suddenly, adults all over England were talking about the pictures and the girls' encounter with the fairies.

ENTER SIR ARTHUR

One of the people most excited about the photos was writer Sir Arthur Conan Doyle. By 1920, he was already famous for his Sherlock Holmes mysteries. He was also well known for his interest in Spiritualism, a religion whose followers believe in the supernatural, especially ghosts. So the fairy photos grabbed his attention.

Doyle never questioned the girls' sincerity, but he did initially question the photos. He showed them to various "fairy experts" (Spiritualists who specialized in identifying fairies). Some of them considered the pictures to be fakes, but others felt they were genuine. Edward Gardner even went to the girls' home with his own camera and asked them to take more pictures to "prove" they'd been right all along. The girls ventured into the woods and returned with more photos of their fairy friends.

Doyle used the original pictures in a magazine article and then, in 1921, wrote a book about the girls and the fairies. Controversy soon exploded on both sides of the fairy fence: Some people were convinced the girls had faked the photos, but they couldn't prove how. Others were sure the pictures were authentic. Either way, the debate continued for many years. Sir Arthur Conan Doyle died in 1930. The girls grew up, married, had children of their own, and eventually became grandmothers. And through the decades, Elsie and Frances stuck to their story.

HAPPILY NEVER AFTER

Then, in 1981, Elsie and Frances finally confessed. The now-elderly women admitted they'd used paper cutouts and pins to pull off the fairy photos. Elsie had copied the images from a popular children's book of the time.

It had all started out as a prank to fool Elsie's mother, they said, but then it got completely out of control. The girls never imagined their pictures would end up circulating all over England, or that they'd be able to fool someone as famous as Sir Arthur Conan Doyle.

Finally, the mystery was solved...or was it? The cousins had come clean about faking the photos, but they always insisted that they really had seen fairies on that long-ago summer day.

*   *   *

"Kids are great. That's one of the best things about pro basketball, all the kids you get to meet. It's a shame they have to grow up to be regular people and come to the games and call you names."   **—Charles Barkley**

On average, twins are born 24 days earlier than single babies.

HOW TO MAKE A SPITBALL

There's so much for kids to learn that we sometimes worry they're forgetting the important things. You may know how to do this, but in case you don't, here are some tips in the art of spitballing.

What you need: Paper, of course, something not too stiff and not too soft. Notebook paper is great. (Hey, you've got plenty of that). You'll also need a lot of spit. (You've got plenty of that, too.)

What to do:

1. Tear off a square piece of paper that's two inches long and two inches wide, and crumple it into a small ball.

2. Stick that paper ball in your mouth. (Don't swallow it.) Chew it up, tenderizing it with your teeth and saliva. You're done when the paper is slimy and saturated with spit, but not quite falling apart.

3. Take it out of your mouth and reshape the paper/spit chunk into a ball by rolling it in the palm of your hand. If it doesn't stay in the ball shape, chew some more.

4. Launch it! The classic way is to put it on your thumb and flick it with your forefinger. You can also stick it into one end of a straw and blow hard in the other end. And please, whatever you do, don't shoot it at your little brother.

Q: What would you get if you crossed a galaxy with a toad? A: Star Warts.

BIZARRE RECORDS

Here at the Bathroom Readers' Institute, we love records—and the weirder, the better. These are some of our favorites.

MOST PINS IN A HUMAN HEAD

In 2004, a Chinese doctor named Wei Sheng stuck 1,790 pins in his head to earn a record for the "most pins in a human head" from *Guinness World Records*. Four years later, to celebrate the 2008 Olympics in Beijing, Sheng pierced his body with 2,008 pins in the five colors of the Olympic rings. Technically, that didn't beat his own record, though, because the 2008 stunt included his head *and* shoulders. Maybe next time.

MOST PEOPLE INSIDE A SOAP BUBBLE

In 2007, Englishman Sam Heath set a world record by gathering 50 elementary school children and encasing them in a giant soap bubble. Heath—who is a professional "bubbleologist," someone who specializes in the science of soap bubbles—built a special wooden wand for the event, and the kids stood on a round platform surrounded by soapy water. He gently dipped the wand in the soap and pulled it around the platform until the 5-foot-tall, 11-foot-wide bubble encircled all the kids.

It wasn't Heath's first attempt at breaking the soapy

record. In 2006, he put 19 children inside a bubble. One of the girls at that event said, "It was really exciting. I really wanted to clap but we had to stay so still."

MOST FINGERS AND TOES

This one's a tie—four-year-old Pranamya Menaria and 14-year-old Devandra Harne, two kids from India, share the title. Both were born with 12 fingers and 13 toes. Having more than 10 fingers and 10 toes is a condition called polydactylism. It affects about 25 percent of people worldwide, but it's not dangerous or deadly.

HEAVIEST CAR BALANCED ON A HUMAN HEAD

Englishman John Evans calls himself a "professional head balancer," but until 1999, he stuck mostly to books and people. However, in May of that year, he earned a world record for balancing a Mini Cooper car (it weighed more than 3,000 pounds) on his head for 33 seconds. Why? He loves to break records and says he'll keep trying for more.

LONGEST FEMALE BEARD

Vivian Wheeler from Illinois holds this record. She was able to grow a beard as a kid, but never did because her dad always encouraged her to shave it off. But in 1993, she stopped shaving, and today her beard is an incredible 11 inches long.

THE REAL RED BARON

*In the Peanuts comics, Snoopy often imagines himself
atop his flying doghouse, battling a fiendish foe called
the Red Baron. But…who was the Red Baron?*

ACE OF ACES

Manfred von Richthofen never intended to be a pilot. Born in 1892 in Germany, he was the son of a Prussian nobleman. His father was in the military, so it made sense that Manfred would be, too. The boy excelled at horseback riding, and when World War I began in 1914, Manfred thought he'd be going to battle on horseback. But mounted soldiers were being replaced by a new vehicle…the airplane.

Von Richthofen enrolled in aviation school and made his first solo flight after only 24 hours of training. He crash landed that first time out, but eventually passed his exams and took to the skies to attack Germany's enemies—the French, Canadians, and English. On September 17, 1916, he shot down his first enemy plane—and began a string of aerial victories that remains unmatched to this day.

THE CRIMSON CRUSADER

By January 14, 1917, von Richthofen had his 16th

victory, making him Germany's number-one flying ace. The German government gave the young pilot a medal and a squadron of his own, which he nicknamed the "Flying Circus." He also painted his plane red—both to intimidate enemies and to make it recognizable to German troops on the ground so they wouldn't shoot at him. Within weeks, his friends and enemies were calling him the Red Baron.

THE FLYING CIRCUS RULES THE SKIES

The Flying Circus became the most feared air squadron in World War I. During "Bloody April" 1917, the British lost 912 airmen to the pilots of the Flying Circus. The Red Baron himself shot down 41 planes. The German military, afraid of losing its best pilot, ordered him to take a couple of months' vacation. But shortly after his return to duty in September, he upped his victory count to 60. By April 1918, the German ace had increased his total to an incredible 80 victories. There seemed no way to stop the Red Baron.

REVENGE OF THE SOPWITH CAMEL

Like most German pilots, von Richthofen usually flew a triplane, which had three wings and was more maneuverable than other airplanes, but didn't always fly steady. In 1916, though, the British air force had introduced a new, sturdier fighter plane, the Sopwith Camel. And it was against one of these that the Red Baron finally met his match.

First character to speak in *Star Wars: A New Hope*: C-3PO.

On April 21, 1918, British pilot Wilfrid May was on patrol over France when he found himself under attack by the Red Baron. May was not an experienced flyer, and he later said that it was because of his erratic, jerky turns that he survived the battle. Nonetheless, the young Englishman held his own.

May finally decided to head back to his own territory, but the German ace followed him. A Canadian pilot named Arthur "Roy" Brown saw the dogfight and chased after von Richthofen's plane, as English and Canadian troops on the ground opened fire. But the Red Baron easily avoided Brown and continued after May, who cringed as machine-gun bullets whipped past his ears.

GOING DOWN

Then suddenly, the firing stopped. May circled back to see the Red Baron's plane making a bouncy emergency landing below. When it came to a stop, English soldiers on the ground approached warily. The plane's motor was still running, and the propeller still turning, but there was no movement in the cockpit. When one of them finally looked inside, he found the Red Baron barely alive. A single bullet had come up through the floor of the plane and lodged in the ace's chest. One of the soldiers on the ground had fired a lucky shot.

The Red Baron died in his cockpit soon after. He was only 25, and legend has it that just before he died, he whispered, "Kaput"—finished.

Number of mammal species identified (so far) by scientists: 5,416.

HOW TO MAKE A VOODOO DOLL

People around the world actually practice voodoo,
but what's the story behind the superstition.

IS VOODOO REAL?

Voodoo is a religion that merges African pagan beliefs and Roman Catholicism. In the 1500s and 1600s, the French (who were mostly Catholic) brought slaves to Haiti from Africa, and those men and women carried their tribal rituals with them. As the two cultures merged, so did the religions. Today, voodoo is an official religion in Haiti and is also widely practiced in Louisiana, where many former Haitian slaves moved in the 18th and 19th centuries.

Many voodoo rituals are based on superstition. Followers believe in spirit possession, the power of dance to cure illness...and voodoo dolls. The dolls can be used for good or bad—their purpose is to affect the lives of the people they represent. And if you've ever wanted to make your own voodoo doll, here's how.

WHAT YOU'LL NEED

Two sticks, moss, string, pieces of fabric (about 12 inches long), yarn that matches your fabric, a needle and thread, fabric glue, buttons, feathers, and scissors.

Fireworks that explode into perfect circles are called "chrysanthemums."

GET STARTED

1. Make a cross with your sticks, and wrap the string around the joint so it's tight. Tie a knot to secure it.

2. Wrap the Spanish moss around the sticks. Start at the joint and then move up and down to create the doll's head and body. Be sure to wrap the moss tightly so that it doesn't fall off; use string to secure it if you need to.

3. Cut the pieces of fabric into two-inch-wide strips and wrap those around the moss. Leave a little moss poking out of each end (for hair, hands, and feet). Glue the end of the last fabric strip to the doll's body.

4. Get the buttons, feathers, needle, and thread. Sew two buttons for eyes and one for the nose. Glue feathers to your doll's head to make hair.

5. Now it's time to personalize your doll. Write the person's initials on the back, and then you're ready to "cast" spells that wish luck or misfortune to the person your doll represents.

EWWW! BOOGERS!

*Lots of people will probably tell you not to
be snotty, but we say, "Go ahead!"*

- About 70 percent of people say they pick their
boogers. (And 3 percent of those admit that they eat
what they pick.)

- Eating your boogers is really gross...but it's not necessarily unhealthy. In fact, because the booger mucus
exposes your body to new and useful bacteria, it can
actually strengthen your immune system. But the
dirty fingers you use to do the picking are full of bad
bacteria that can make you sick.

- Eye boogers (those round balls of mucus that collect
in the corners of your eyes and sometimes turn
crusty) are made from the same stuff as the boogers in
your nose.

- Pure boogers are clear.

- You get especially snotty in cold weather because
when the temperature drops, your body produces
more mucus to line your throat and nose. In the cold
air, the mucus is usually thick. But when you go
inside someplace warm, it thins and drips out.

- Animals make boogers, too. If horses get stuffy, they
just take a deep breath and blow hard through their
noses. Other animals, like bison, have tongues long
enough to lick their noses clean.

WHO SAID THAT?

Want to learn to speak without moving your lips?

TALK LIKE A DUMMY
Ventriloquism got its start hundreds of years ago as a way (some people believed) to talk to the dead. Ventriloquists were considered to be prophets, and supposedly, spirits slipped into their stomachs and spoke from there. The word *ventriloquism* even comes from Latin words that mean "belly speaker." Of course, the spirits weren't really talking—it was the ventriloquist manipulating his voice to fool the audience.

Today, ventriloquists make it sound like their voices are coming from a puppet. Ventriloquism isn't easy, but if you work at it, you can do it just as well as the professionals.

KEEP YOUR MOUTH SHUT!
Ventriloquists use two main tricks. The first is misdirection. When the ventriloquist's puppet is "speaking," the audience focuses on it. That distracts people from watching the ventriloquist, or noticing if he makes a mistake.

A ventriloquist's second trick is to alter his speech to mask difficult sounds. Most letter sounds are easy. Hold your mouth slightly open and recite the alphabet. Most of the letters require no or minimal use of your lips. The ones that you do have to move your lips to pronounce are B, F, M, P, Q, V, and W. So what's a budding ventriloquist to do? You can't just avoid those letters altogether.

FAKE OUT

Try these substitutions:

- For "B," say "geh," which comes from the back of your throat instead of your lips. For example, instead of "bottle," you'd say "gottle."

- For "F" and "V," take a tip from Daffy Duck. Replace either sound with "th." In other words, things aren't "very fantastic," they're "thery thantastic."

- "M" is easy, just use an "N" sound. If your dummy calls you a "moron," don't be offended—he actually said "noron."

- "P" can be tricky. "P" or "puh" is replaced by a "kuh" or "kluh" from the back of your throat. Example: "They pay you to write these jokes?" would become "They kay you to write these jokes?"

- A "Q" is really made up of two different sounds: the "cuh" and the "oo." For ventriloquism, mash the two sounds together to make a lipless "koo" sound, as in "koo-iet" for "quiet."

- The "wuh" of a "W" can be covered up with an "ooo" or "oh," as in "oo-ut's going on?"

Now all you need is kuh-ractice!

LET ME OUTTA HERE!

Papillon—which means "butterfly" in French—was the nickname of a man named Henri Charrière. It's also the title of his book and of a movie based on his story of life in prison and daring escape. But how much of his tale is actually true?

HENRI'S STORY

In 1931, 25-year-old Frenchman Henri Charrière was convicted of murder and given a life sentence of hard labor. In those days, France sent its convicted criminals to French Guiana, a small territory that sits on the north coast of South America. Most of the cells in the prison were reserved for violent criminals, and Charrière certainly qualified. (Fellow prisoners called him "Papillon" or "Papi" because he had a tattoo of a butterfly on his chest.) He always swore that he wasn't guilty, and vowed to escape the unjust punishment no matter the cost.

ON THE RUN

As soon as he arrived, Charrière started plotting his escape. The first time, he knocked out a guard in the prison's hospital and made it all the way to Colombia. But he was caught and imprisoned there.

Before he could be sent back to French Guiana, he used a hacksaw to cut through the bars of his cell. (He'd bought the saw secretly from some men who sneaked it into the Colombian prison.) That time, he managed to live on the run for a few months before he was recaptured. Then it was back to French Guiana and two years of solitary confinement as punishment.

DEVIL'S ISLAND

Eventually, Charrière ended up at the most isolated prison in French Guiana. Called Devil's Island, this brutal prison was just offshore, and prisoners there were beaten and poorly fed. Deadly diseases like malaria were rampant, and the jungle around the prison was filled with fire ants and other dangerous creatures. From 1852 (when the prison opened) until 1946 (when it closed), about 80,000 prisoners died on Devil's Island.

But still, Charrière tried to escape. He made a raft from coconut shells and, one night, jumped from a cliff into the ocean. Floating on his raft, he managed to get to land and, with the help of strangers, trav-

The East Indian wandering whistling duck whistles rather than quacks.

eled all the way to Venezuela. The authorities there captured him, but refused to return him to Devil's Island. According to them, it was too violent a place. So in 1945, after 14 years and a total of nine escapes, Charrière was a free man. He settled in Venezuela, got married, had children, opened a restaurant, and wrote his autobiography.

THE TRICKY PART

But was it really *his* biography? When Charrière's book was published in 1969, it was an immediate success. People all over the world were fascinated by his tale. But decades later, in 2005, another prisoner from Devil's Island claimed that *he* was the real Papillon.

Charles Brunier was 104 years old and living in a nursing home outside of Paris. He said he'd known Henri Charrière back in the 1930s and 1940s, when they were both imprisoned in French Guiana. Brunier claimed that he told Charrière stories of three of his own escapes, all of which appear in the book. Brunier even had his own butterfly tattoo—on his left arm.

History seems to back up Brunier's story. Other prisoners remembered seeing him on Devil's Island. Some also remembered Charrière. But they said he wasn't an escape artist and had a reputation as a model prisoner. Others even said Charrière was never at Devil's Island at all. The prison didn't keep good records of who came and went, so we'll probably never know for sure who the real Papillon was. Henri Charrière died in 1973.

SPOT OF MYSTERY

*Can there really be a place where the laws
of time and gravity don't apply?*

S TRANGE HOUSE IN THE WOODS
In 1890, Gold Hill, Oregon, was a small, sleepy
town with little gold left to mine. That year, after
a heavy rainstorm, a former gold processing office (basically, a shack on a hill in the forest) slid off of its foun-
dation and came to rest farther down the hillside.
People went inside and found a place that didn't seem
to make any sense: rocks rolled uphill, and people were
able to stand on the walls.

In 1930, that shack—now called the Oregon Vortex
House of Mystery—opened as a tourist attraction where
visitors could see the strangeness for themselves:

• Brooms stand on end.

• Children appear taller than adults.

• And few animals seemed willing to enter the area.

But how...and why?

BRING IN THE SCIENTIST

John Lister was an engineer from England. He came to
the Vortex in 1929 to study all the strange goings-on.
He even discussed what he called "abnormalities" in the
area's magnetic field with Albert Einstein.

...Top-selling gift for Christmas, 2005: Sony's PlayStation 3.

Lister seemed to think there was something extraordinary happening, but he never shared his findings with anyone. To this day, no one really knows what he came up with. Legend has it that, before he died in 1959, he burned all his notes, but supposedly, he'd written, "The world isn't yet ready for what goes on here."

SO WHAT'S REALLY GOING ON?

Over the years, people came up with many different theories:

1. When the house fell, it moved so fast that it ripped a hole in the earth and created a "gravitational anomaly," where "high-velocity soft electrons" exit the earth. (Not likely, because there are no such things as "gravitational anomalies" or "high-velocity soft electrons.")

2. There's a giant underground magnet or other device that's causing the strange activity. (Also unlikely.)

3. The weirdness could be caused by magnetic rocks in the area. (Possible, but there is no evidence of iron or other magnetic rocks in the ground near Gold Hill.)

4. High concentrations of volcanic rocks cause the strange events. (Not true—volcanic rocks can't alter gravity.)

THE EXPLANATION?

The debate has raged for years. True believers always point to magnetic abnormalities, or even the supernat-

---

Studies show: The three most dangerous foods to eat in a car are coffee, tacos, and chili.

ural. But most people think the tricks at the Vortex are just optical illusions. The House of Mystery is likely a tilted house at a strange incline on a hill. The floor, walls, and ceiling are built at sloping angles to trick people's brains into thinking everything looks crooked and distorted.

There are similar "mystery spots" all over the United States. Almost all of them (like the Oregon Vortex) opened in the 1930s as cheap roadside attraction to thrill Depression-era travelers. Most of them have a similar hook: single-room shacks on a hillside that are "beyond the realm of science." Check out one near you...if you dare:

- The Mystery Spot: Santa Cruz, California
- Confusion Hill: Piercy, California
- The Mystery Spot: St. Ignace, Michigan
- The Mystery Hill: Marblehead, Ohio
- The Mystery Shack: Maggie Valley, North Carolina
- Spook Hill: Lake Wales, Florida
- Cosmos of the Black Hills: Rapid City, South Dakota
- Gravity Hill: Bedford County, Pennsylvania

*　　*　　*

COWBOY PROVERB
Never dig for water under an outhouse.

First job: Patrick Dempsey of *Grey's Anatomy* worked as a unicycle-riding clown.

REAL TREASURE HUNTING

*Want to go looking for treasure? Well, ye pirate, here's one
of the Caribbean's most notorious stashes. So attach
your peg leg, raise your Jolly Roger, and cast off!*

SEEKING: 55 chests of silver and gold
LAST SEEN ON...Norman Island in the British
Virgin Islands, which some people say was the
setting for Robert Louis Stevenson's novel
Treasure Island.

THE LEGEND: In 1750, a ship called *Nuestra Senora
de Guádelope* was bound for Spain and carrying a fortune in gold, silver, and spices. Somewhere in the
Atlantic, either the crew mutinied or pirates took
over—no one knows for sure—and half of the
cargo was lost at sea. Englishman Owen Lloyd,
a member of the *Guádelope's* crew, stole the
other half, loaded it onto his own
ship, and sailed 1,000 miles
to the British Virgin Islands
in the Caribbean Sea.
Lloyd and his cohorts
stashed chests of gold and
silver on the uninhabited
Norman Island, named after a

pirate who retired there with his spoils in the early
1700s. But Lloyd never got a chance to do that—he
and his gang were captured before they could retrieve
the goods.

People on nearby Tortola Island saw Lloyd's ship and
heard his buddies brag about the hidden booty. So the
locals put two and two together and
rushed to Norman Island. They
discovered
the loot, but
the British
government soon
found them and took
the treasure.

But did they
find all of it?
Around 1910, a
fisherman caught in a storm took shelter in a cave on
Norman Island. Waves slammed his boat against the
rocks all night. Local legend claims that he woke up
the next morning to find chunks of rock in his boat
along with a surprise—a small chest of gold coins. He
never officially reported the discovery, so the story
can't be confirmed. But people who live nearby believe
the man used the money to open several tourist shops
around town. So treasure-seekers still travel to the area
and continue the hunt for the remaining chests.

*To read about more sunken treasure, steer your
ship over to page 97.*

To read about more sunken treasure, steer your ship over to page 97.

Charles Darwin was born on the same day as Abraham Lincoln—February 12, 1809.

GO TO COLLEGE FOR FREE!

If you meet some rather strange requirements, maybe you can get one of these scholarships.

THE ZOLP SCHOLARSHIP

Who's eligible? Anyone who's attending Loyola University in Chicago, Illinois, who is Catholic, and...whose last name is Zolp.

KLINGON LANGUAGE INSTITUTE AWARD

Who's eligible? It's open to anyone who studies languages—speaking fluent Klingon (an alien language on *Star Trek*) is not a requirement.

FREDERICK AND MARY F. BECKLEY SCHOLARSHIP

Who's eligible? Anyone who's left-handed and attends Juniata College in Pennsylvania.

CARNEGIE MELLON UNIVERSITY BAGPIPE SCHOLARSHIP

Who's eligible? Anyone majoring in bagpipes at Pittsburgh's Carnegie Mellon University. As of 2009, though, there was only one bagpipe major in the United States. (His name is Nick Hudson.)

Misnamed times two: Pineapples don't contain pine *or* apples.

NATIONAL BEEF AMBASSADOR PROGRAM

Who's eligible? Applicants have to give a speech and ace several interview questions...about beef. The top five get scholarships.

PATRICK KERR SKATEBOARD SCHOLARSHIP

Who's eligible? Must have a GPA of at least 2.5 and be an avid skateboarder. (Those unfamiliar with the terms "kickflip" and "boardslide" need not apply.)

TALL CLUBS INTERNATIONAL SCHOLARSHIP

Who's eligible? Men who are taller than 6'2", and women taller than 5'10".

*   *   *

NOTHING GETS PAST HIM

In February 2009, Kansas high school senior Geoffrey Stanford found a major error on his state's standardized English exam. The test writers had used the word "omission" in a question about carbon dioxide, when they really meant to say "emission." Geoffrey showed the mistake to his teacher, who passed it on to the board of education; they fixed it. As for Geoffrey, he's not surprised he noticed the error. He says, "When I edit my own papers, I'm a stickler for...the correct use of words. It annoys me when I see mistakes."

TOON-EMIES

Even cartoon characters can be annoyed. Can you match these mischievous kids with their enemies? (Answers on page 241.)

1. Bart Simpson
2. SpongeBob SquarePants
3. Flapjack
4. Johnny Test
5. Timmy Turner
6. Jake Long
7. The Mighty B
8. Charlie Brown
9. Kim Possible
10. Aang (Avatar)
11. Powerpuff Girls
12. Ben 10
13. Chowder
14. Lazlo
15. Jimmy Neutron
16. Jason Fox

a) Icky Vicky
b) Scoutmaster Lumpus
c) Plankton
d) Eight-Armed Willy
e) The Huntsman
f) Portia Gibbons
g) Lucy Van Pelt
h) Paige Fox
i) Gorgonzola
j) Mojo Jojo
l) Nelson Muntz
n) Vilgax
o) Doctor Drakken
p) The Fire Lord
q) Bling-Bling Boy
r) Cindy Vortex

Q. Who is Hannah Montana's rude rival? A: Mikayla.

FREETHINKERS

Whose beat do you march to?

"You have to expect things of yourself before you can do them."
—**Michael Jordan**

"Be who you are and say what you feel because those who mind don't matter and those who matter don't mind."
—**Dr. Seuss**

"The only rule is don't be boring, and dress cute wherever you go. Life is too short to blend in."
—**Paris Hilton**

"Look, Your Worshipfulness, let's get one thing straight. I take orders from just one person: me."
—**Han Solo,** *Star Wars*

"I just write what I want to write. I write what amuses me. It's totally for myself."
—**J. K. Rowling**

"Doubt everything. Find your own light."
—**Buddha**

"Procrastination isn't the problem; it's the solution. So procrastinate now, don't put it off.
—**Ellen DeGeneres**

"You alone are enough."
—**Oprah Winfrey**

"Some people march to a different drummer— and some people polka."
—**Uncle John**

ASK THE EXPERTS

Raise your hand...and ask these questions.
We bet they'll make your teacher's head spin.

Q. Why do we drive on a parkway but park on a driveway?
A: A "parkway" doesn't refer to parked vehicles; originally, parkways were roads that went through or connected public parks. In the 1800s, driveways were private roads that horse-drawn carriages used to travel from the main street to a house or garage. But today, space is more limited, so driveways are shorter and are often used to park vehicles.

Q. Why do drive-up ATMs include Braille writing if blind people don't drive?
A: Visually impaired people do use walk-up ATMs, and the law requires that banks have machines they can use. It's cheaper to install the same keypads used on walk-up ATMs in the drive-up ones than it is to make new, Braille-less keypads.

Q. Why do airplanes have flotation devices, but not parachutes, under their seats?
A: Commercial planes fly too high and too fast for someone to survive a parachute jump. Some jets soar over 40,000 feet, where there's not enough oxygen in

Australian toilets don't swirl counterclockwise when flushed...

the air to breathe. Even at a lower altitude, skydiving passengers probably couldn't clear the plane's wings. And if they did manage to do so, it's doubtful they could steer their parachutes and land safely without training. So, because passengers are a lot more likely to survive a water landing than a parachute jump, planes contain flotation cushions.

Q. Why do stores that are open 24 hours a day, 365 days a year, have locks on their doors?

A: Mostly it's in case of an emergency; store employees may need to lock themselves inside for protection.

Also, most commercial buildings do need locks on their doors, and like the ATMs, it costs less to make a lot of doors with the same features than it does to make special ones for 24-hour stores.

Q. My dad says "flammable" and "inflammable" are opposites. Is he right?

A: No. Both words mean "easily set on fire." The word "inflammable" was first used in the early 17th century, and since then, it has caused a lot of confusion. The prefix "in-" sometimes means "not," so people have often thought things labeled "inflammable" were fireproof when they weren't.

In the 20th century, scientists, firefighters, and insurance companies agreed to start using the word "flammable" and its opposite, "nonflammable," to make things more clear.

THEY WERE AHEAD OF THEIR TIME

Being annoying and pushy can get you far in life…as it did for these two women who stood up to prejudice and made people take them seriously.

ANNE HUTCHINSON

In 1634, when she was 43 years old, Anne Hutchinson left England and moved with her husband and children to the Massachusetts colony in North America. Despite the fact that she wasn't an ordained minister, she started giving sermons and organized Bible study groups for women in Boston. They'd get together and talk about religious verses or ideas, and Hutchinson usually offered her own thoughts. Often her ideas differed from the ones taught in English churches, especially when it came to the rights of women and minorities. Hutchinson believed that the Bible said they were equal to white men; the church disagreed.

By 1637, Anne Hutchinson's study groups were full of women and men, and the official church of Massachusetts (the Puritan church) had labeled her a "troublemaker." The next year, the colony put her on trial for heresy, or speaking out against the established beliefs of the church.

At her trial, Hutchinson refused to back down. She challenged the judges and defended her right to hold her meetings. The judges, though, were having none of it; they banished her from Massachusetts.

So she moved to Rhode Island, which had become a place in the colonies known for being tolerant of different ideas. Hutchinson helped establish the colony's government and continued giving lectures and holding her Bible study meetings. She was also one of many inspirations for William Penn, who founded the Pennsylvania colony in 1681 and created a government based on equality and religious tolerance. Eventually Anne Hutchinson moved to New York and died there in 1643.

It took a long time, but the State of Massachusetts finally changed its mind about Anne Hutchinson. Today, more than 300 years after her death, she's got a statue outside the statehouse. The inscription on it calls her a "courageous exponent [advocate] of civil liberty and religious toleration."

AMELIA BLOOMER

What did women in the 1800s wear under their dresses? Before Amelia Bloomer came along, they had only restrictive underwear that made it difficult for them to play sports or ride bicycles. But thanks to Bloomer's innovation—a pair of puffy pants that gathered around the ankles with elastic—women could be a lot more comfortable.

Bloomer didn't start out as a feminist. Her first cause was temperance, a movement in the mid-19th century to ban alcohol in the United States. But by 1849, she'd started her own newspaper, the first in the United States to be produced entirely by and for women. She also started giving speeches about women's rights, and when she showed up for an event, she often wore puffy trousers under a short skirt. But pants were considered men's clothing, and at the time, Bloomer was ridiculed for wearing something so odd. She kept doing it, though, and to make fun of her, men started calling the pants "bloomers."

But bloomers eventually caught on with women. By the 1890s (around the time Bloomer died in 1894), bicycling became a trendy hobby among men and women in the United States. And women—who had a hard time maneuvering their bicycles while wearing long skirts and tight undergarments—started wearing bloomers and short skirts...just like Amelia Bloomer had. It would be more than 50 years before it became commonplace to see women wearing pants, but bloomers became an acceptable way for women to be comfortable and fashionable at the same time.

*   *   *

"I pick my nose and I'm not ashamed to admit it. If there's a [booger], then just pick it, man."

—**Justin Timberlake**

Q. What goes around the world but stays in a corner? A. A stamp

THE CASE OF THE KIDNAPPED KID

When Uncle John heard this tale, he immediately called in his favorite detective—Inspector Commodius Loo—to solve the crime. See if you can figure it out. (Answer on page 241.)

HEAD GAMES

One of Miss Shapen's students, Winslow, had been kidnapped. Winslow's dad paid the $20,000 ransom, but things hadn't gone as planned. Winslow was still missing, and his brother Waldo—who had delivered a gym bag full of cash to the ransom drop—was suffering from a bump on his head.

"I went to the deserted parking garage just like they told me," Waldo said to Inspector Loo. "But somebody conked me on the back of the head. I fell and dropped the gym bag. My attacker swooped in from behind, picked it up, and ran off. I never saw his face, only his back. He was tall and redheaded, wearing jeans and a zippered sweat-shirt—it might have had a college logo, I'm not sure."

"Anyone else around?" Loo asked.

"A homeless guy showed up, pushing a shopping cart," Waldo said. "Then someone drove up in a Mer-cedes. He wanted to call the cops, but I begged him not to. The kidnappers said no police."

"Now they want another $20,000," Miss Shapen wailed. "What should we do? Should we track down the homeless man and the Mercedes driver?"

"No need," Loo said. "I know what happened."

How did Inspector Loo crack the case, and what had he figured out?

*   *   *

BLOWIN' IN THE WIND

In 2009, people living next door to folk rocker Bob Dylan in Malibu, California, had a complaint: the portable toilet he kept on his property stank. (The singer had hired construction workers to do some renovating, and they needed a place to go.) Dylan's next-door neighbors said the toilet smelled so bad that it made them sick. When complaints to the city didn't work, they came up with their own solution: they installed huge fans on their deck and blew the stink back at Dylan's house.

BAD WORDS

*Here are the origins to some real words that are
acceptable to say, but sound naughty anyway.*

URANUS. In 1781, astronomer William Herschel
called this planet Georgium Sidus, after King George III
of England. But since all of the other planets were
named after ancient gods, German astronomer J. E.
Bode renamed it after Ouranos, the Greek god of the
sky. And the correct pronunciation is not "yer-anus,"
but the much more respectable sounding "urine-us."

WINNIE THE POOH. This was the name of a teddy
bear owned by Christopher Robin Milne, the son of
author A. A. Milne. He named it Winnie after a bear at
the London Zoo, and Pooh after a swan the family had
met while on vacation. (No word on why they chose to
name a swan after you-know-what.)

RECTIFY. This word, meaning "to make right something that is wrong," sounds like it should have a
naughty origin, but sadly, it doesn't. It comes from the
Latin *rectificare*, which means "to make right." Yawn.

TITMOUSE. The name for this bird species comes
from two Old English words—*tyt* meant "little," and
mase meant "bird." Over the centuries, *tytmase* turned
into "titmouse." *Warning:* Only experienced bird watch-
ers can say this word without cracking themselves up.

"Big sisters are the crab grass in the lawn of life." —Charles M. Schulz

RIDE 'EM, COWGIRL!

What if the winner of a contest to find America's greatest cowboy was...a girl?

MOVE OVER, BOYS
In 1904, the best cowboys in the Southwest gathered together to compete in a roping competition in Dennison, Texas. A lot was on the line: $10,000 in prize money (a fortune in those days) and the title of "World's Greatest Roper." But no one paid much attention to one of the competitors, an 18-year-old girl from Oklahoma. Back then, very few women participated in rodeo competitions along with the men, and no one thought this girl, with her slight frame and refined manners, was likely to win anything. It was the last time anyone made that mistake.

When her chance came, Lucille Mulhall roped three steers in 3 minutes, 36 seconds. No other rider could match her, and when the dust cleared, Mulhall had earned the gold medal, the world record, and the $10,000 prize.

A STAR IS BORN

Word spread about the Oklahoman, and the following year, Mulhall was the main attraction in a star-studded rodeo at New York City's Madison Square Garden. President Teddy Roosevelt was so dazzled by her roping and riding that he declared her "the world's most expert horsewoman." But it was a fellow Oklahoman—a performer and champion rider—named Will Rogers who gave her the nickname that stuck: "America's First Cowgirl." According to Rogers, the word "cowgirl" had never been used before Lucille Mulhall came along.

BRED IN THE SADDLE

Mulhall was born in 1885 and, as she told a reporter later, "I've ridden all my life. I expect my father gave me a horseback ride before I was a month old." Her father was Zack Mulhall, an army colonel and rancher who owned more than 82,000 acres in Oklahoma. Young 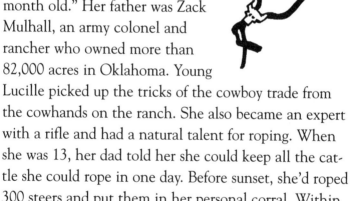 Lucille picked up the tricks of the cowboy trade from the cowhands on the ranch. She also became an expert with a rifle and had a natural talent for roping. When she was 13, her dad told her she could keep all the cattle she could rope in one day. Before sunset, she'd roped 300 steers and put them in her personal corral. Within days, her herd grew to more than 1,000, and her father was forced to call off the deal.

SWEETHEART OF THE RODEO

Mulhall got her start in show business in 1899 when her dad took her to the St. Louis World's Fair to star in his Wild West Show called "The Congress of Rough Riders and Ropers." People there were amazed that such a small person (she was only five feet tall) could rope and wrestle huge steers to the ground. But Mulhall was whipcord-strong, and she worked as a headliner in rodeos and Wild West shows across the United States and around the world until 1917.

THE GOVERNOR

When she wasn't starring in rodeos, Mulhall trained hundreds of horses, but her favorite was named Governor. She taught him to do more than 40 tricks, including shooting a gun, pulling off a man's coat, and walking up and down stairs. Governor was so skilled that Mulhall joked, "He has received a good education, and does nearly everything but talk."

END OF THE TRAIL

When World War I put an end to the heyday of Wild West shows, Mulhall went back to the family ranch in Oklahoma. She lived there until 1940, when she died in a car crash. She was inducted into the Cowboy Hall of Fame in 1975, and to the Cowgirl Hall of Fame in 1977. Both places gave her the title "All-Around Champion Cowgirl."

* * *

Slip 'n Slide: Ice isn't actually slippery. Things slip on ice because a thin layer of ice melts when pressure is applied to it. That wet layer is what's slippery.

THE PRESIDENTS' REPORT CARDS

Someone as successful as the president of the United States probably earned straight As from kindergarten through college, right? Not necessarily.

- **Woodrow Wilson's** teachers labeled him a "slow learner" because he was unable to read well until he was 11 years old. Yet Wilson went on to be the only president to date who earned a PhD.

- **John F. Kennedy's** sixth-grade teacher said that he was only an average student, and that his weakest subjects were spelling, science, and math. Two of his report cards from 1930 (when he was 13) show he struggled with foreign languages, too: at one school, he earned a D in French, and at another, a 64 percent average in Latin. One of his teachers wrote, "He can do better than this."

- **Andrew Johnson** didn't go to school at all, and didn't learn to read or write until he was 17 years old.

- **George H. W. Bush** got many Cs in school, and some of his

The polecat is not a cat. It's a weasel.

teachers were unimpressed with his intelligence. One said, "He just sat in class and handed in papers...He showed no imagination or originality."

- **Ulysses S. Grant** went to the U.S. Military Academy at West Point in 1839, but only because his father made him go. Grant wanted to be a tanner, someone who makes leather, not the military man his father wanted him to be. He struggled with the school's math-heavy curriculum, but finally graduated in 1843, with a C average.

THE HIGH SCORERS

Not all U.S. presidents struggled in school, though. Bill Clinton's classmates said that the only mystery about his grades was whether "he'd get a high A or a low A." And Barack Obama's fifth-grade teacher called him "a really smart student."

*　　*　　*

PRESIDENTIAL WISE GUY

One president definitely left an impression—not for his grades, but for his antics. According to his teachers, George W. Bush was a handful. He once threw a football through a school window, and in fourth grade, he entertained his classmates by "drawing an ink moustache, goatee, and sideburns on himself." That earned him a trip to the principal's office.

Mmmm...BRAINS

Q: Why do zombies eat brains? A: Because they taste good. Here are some more brainy facts.

- The average human brain weighs three pounds. (For comparison, all of your skin weighs about six pounds.)

- Animals (including people) yawn to wake up their brains. When you're tired or bored, your brain becomes less alert. Yawning brings a lot of oxygen into your body quickly, and that stimulates your brain.

- The brain uses up about 20 percent of the blood and oxygen in the human body.

- Your brain cannot feel pain because there are no nerves in it. That's why neurosurgeons can poke around in the brains of patients who are awake. (A headache is caused by pain in the nerves and muscles in your neck and skull, not a pain in the brain.)

- Your brain is made up of about 75 percent water. The rest is mostly protein and fat.

- Some animals—like sponges, jellyfish, and starfish—don't have a brain.

- The human brain keeps growing until a person is about 18 years old.

- If you could spread your brain out flat, it would be the width of a pillowcase.

- Your brain is about the same consistency as Jell-O.

STING AND BITE

*If you're the student who'd be voted "most likely
to put a rubber spider on your teacher's
desk," you might like these creatures.*

JUST SHOOT ME!

There's a good reason that the bullet ant, found in South American rain forests, is called that—people say getting stung by one of these creatures hurts as badly as getting shot. Biologists rate insect stings from 0 to 4 on the Sting Pain Index. A honeybee sting rates about a 2, but the bullet ant is a 4+! A bullet-ant sting won't kill you, but you may feel nauseous, with burning and throbbing at the spot of the sting. And the pain can last for up to 24 hours.

But for many boys of the Satere-Mawe tribe in Brazil, the agonizing bullet-ant sting is just a part of growing up. During a ceremony that marks the passage from boyhood to manhood, many young tribesmen stick their hands into gloves filled with about 400 bullet ants—and their hands stay in the gloves for a full 10 minutes. After going through the ritual 20 times over the course of many months, the boys arc finally considered men.

EIGHT-LEGGED DEATH

Bullet ants are wimps compared to the Sydney funnel-web spider—this creature can kill you in as little as 15 minutes. Often considered the world's deadliest spider,

A bidet is a toilet-sized sink used for washing your behind.

the funnel-web's fangs look kind of like a cat's claws, except that they're also coated with a deadly poison. When threatened, the funnel-web stands up on its back legs and bares its fangs. And those chompers are powerful. Bites have been known to pierce a person's toenails. Once bitten, victims can expect to experience pain, drooling, vomiting, sweating, and unconsciousness, and the male funnel-webs are more dangerous than females. Not only that, but the spiders' venom seems to affect apes, monkeys, and humans more than other mammals. Fortunately, an antidote is now available to counteract the funnel-web's bite.

SWIMMERS BEWARE

Bearded fireworms grow to be between two and six inches long, and they slither underwater along reefs and under rocks, mostly in the Atlantic Ocean. They're slow, so they only pose a threat to humans who touch them. These worms are colorful creatures (usually bright orange) and are covered with fuzzy white bristles. They look cool, but their bristles are full of poison that will burn your skin. And the pain lasts for days, so if you're exploring tidepools along the coast and you see a pretty, fuzzy worm, you might want to admire it from a distance.

WRONG FACTS

Just because you learned it in school doesn't make it true.

FACT? *Abraham Lincoln freed the slaves.*

WRONG! In 1862, in the middle of the Civil War, President Lincoln issued the Emancipation Proclamation, an executive order that made slavery illegal in the United States. But it didn't really accomplish much. Slavery was already illegal in the North. In the South, where it was legal, the states had withdrawn from the country, igniting the Civil War. The Emancipation Proclamation specifically banned slavery in the southern states, which Lincoln no longer had authority over. Slavery wasn't officially outlawed until the passage of the 13th Amendment to the Constitution in December 1865, after the end of the Civil War, the reinstatement of the southern states, and Lincoln's death.

FACT? *Slavery is illegal in the United States.*
WRONG! The 13th Amendment banned the private ownership of slaves and the practice of slavery. But slavery isn't absolutely illegal. It's never been acted upon, but according to the 13th Amendment, the federal government can still make someone a slave as a punishment for a crime. And get this: Mississippi didn't approve the 13th Amendment until 1994, meaning it was legal to own slaves there until that time. (Nobody actually did, though.)

THUMPER MEETS BUMPER

*Tired of the same old cafeteria lunch? Try
one of these food festivals or cook-offs.*

Food Festival: Waurika Rattlesnake Hunt
Location: Waurika, Oklahoma
Explanation: Contestants compete for a $150
prize for the longest rattlesnake caught in the woods.
Afterward, everybody eats deep-fried rattlesnake (which
tastes like stringy chicken).

Food Festival: The Roadkill Cook-off
Location: Marlintown, West Virginia
Explanation: Each September, chefs gather to cook
"found" meat. Don't worry—people aren't running over
animals just so they can cook them. In fact, the festival
doesn't even allow "actual" roadkill, just the meat of
animals most commonly killed in traffic. Past winners
include "Stir-Tired Possum," "Rigormortis Bear Stew,"
and "Thumper Meets Bumper."

Most of the sweaters Mr. Rogers wore on TV were knitted by his mother.

Food Festival: National Baby Food Festival
Location: Fremont, Michigan
Explanation: Fremont is the home of Gerber, the world's largest baby food manufacturer. Every July, the city and company hold this festival, which includes a baby crawl race, a baby food speed-eating contest (for adults) in which two people simultaneously feed each other five jars of food, and a cooking contest in which some of the ingredients have to be Gerber baby food.

Food Festival: Waikiki Spam Jam
Location: Waikiki, Hawaii

Explanation: Spam (it's mostly ham, pork shoulder, and spices) is extremely popular in Hawaii. American troops introduced it to the islands during World War II, and the people there embraced it. Today, Hawaii consumes more Spam than any other state, and it's such a part of the culture that it has its own festival. Past dishes have included barbecue Spam, seaweed-wrapped Spam, and Spam pizza. Don't forget to get your picture taken with the walking Spam-can!

Food Festival: Gilroy Garlic Festival
Location: Gilroy, California
Explanation: More than 2,000 tons of garlic are used to feed the festival's 20,000 visitors, who feast on garlic bread and pasta, garlic chocolate, and garlic ice cream.

THE GREAT RAILROAD RUSE

For many years, history books said that the first railroad to cross the United States was completed in Utah in 1869. The National Park Service even has a historic site there dedicated to the event. But we investigated and found out that it didn't happen quite the way most people believe.

THE TALE THAT'S OFTEN TOLD

American politicians had been wanting to connect the East Coast with the West since the 1840s, when gold was discovered in California and Oregon. That event brought a stampede: thousands of people crossed the United States, hoping to find their fortunes. But pioneers could get only as far as Missouri by train; they had to take a covered wagon or stagecoach the rest of the way. That took a long time (up to six months), and it was dangerous. The travelers could be attacked, robbed, or even killed by outlaws or Indians. So by the 1860s, the government had decided to build a transcontinental railroad across the United States. Actually, they decided to build *two* railroads—one heading west from Omaha, Nebraska, and the other going east from Sacramento, California. And the plan was that they'd meet in the middle.

Construction officially began in 1865, and four years later, the two lines met in Promontory Summit, Utah.

On May 10, 1869, the railroad companies invited newspaper reporters to a celebration and marked the occasion by pounding in a golden spike, which connected the two ends of the line.

THAT'S REALLY GREAT, BUT...

It *is* true that on May 10, 1869, the two lines met in Utah and joined together to create one long railroad line. But the railroad was not "transcontinental"—it didn't cross the entire continent. It only ran from Omaha to Sacramento; travelers still had to ride in stagecoaches from Sacramento to San Francisco (about 87 miles) to reach the Pacific Ocean. And to get to the Atlantic from Omaha, they had to get off the train, cross the Missouri River by boat, and then get on another train to the eastern cities.

In November 1869, a rail line from Sacramento to San Francisco opened. But it wasn't until August 1870 that the first true cross-country railroad was completed. It connected the Sacramento–Omaha line to an East Coast railroad. Finally, people could ride one train from the Atlantic Ocean to the Pacific.

TRANSCONTINENTAL FACTS

- It cost more than $50 million to build all the lines of the Transcontinental Railroad.

- Chinese immigrants made up the majority of the workforce. By the time the railroad was completed, more than 11,000 Chinese laborers had worked on it.

They weren't paid very well, though, only about $25 a month. (White workers made $35 per month.)

- The Sacramento–Omaha line was supposed to have been completed on May 8, but bad weather and arguing between workers and managers held things up. The newspaper reporters who'd been invited to the golden spike ceremony didn't want to wait to write their stories, though—some other news item might come in, and they'd need the time for that. So by May 10, many reporters had already written their accounts of the event, even though few of them actually saw it.

- No one "pounded in" a golden spike to connect the Sacramento–Omaha. There were two golden spikes crafted just for the ceremony, and some railroad company bigwigs gently tapped them into holes in the rails with a silver hammer. But both spikes were immediately removed and replaced with iron ones so they wouldn't be damaged.

- In 1869, if you wanted to travel first-class across the country in a sleeper car (a train's most comfortable accommodations), the five-day trip on the Transcontinental Railroad cost $150 per person.

*　　*　　*

BIG APPETITE

President Theodore Roosevelt often ate 12 eggs for breakfast.

COOL CARD TRICKS

Not only is Uncle John the King of the Throne Room, he's also a master of card tricks. These two always amaze the crowd.

ALL HANDS ON DECK
Setting up: Get one deck of cards. Hold the deck in your hands. Make sure all the cards are facedown. Then flip the bottom card over so that, if you turn the deck upside down, it looks like the top card.

1. Now, gather an audience. Hold all the cards facedown. Fan out the deck, and have someone pick a card. Make sure you keep holding the rest of the cards.

2. Turn your back as your friend shows his card to everyone else. Make sure you do not see the card.

3. While the group is looking at the card, flip the deck over. Since you already slipped the bottom card upside down, when you turn the deck over, that bottom card will look like the one on the top.

4. Have your friend put his card back in the deck. (Be very careful that no one sees that most of the cards are facing the wrong way.) When your buddy puts the card back in, it will be the only one flipped that way.

5. Search the deck and find the card. (Again, do it carefully so that no one sees that most of the cards are facing the wrong way.) When you find it, show it to your audience and watch their jaws drop!

BLACKS AND REDS

Setting up: Before you perform this trick, take a full deck of cards and separate it into two piles: one with the red cards, and one with the black. Place the two piles facedown on a table.

1. Bring in your audience. Ask a friend to choose one card from each pile. Tell her to memorize the cards and remember which pile they came from. Next, ask her to put the cards anywhere she wants in the opposite pile.

2. Ask another friend to shuffle each pile separately, keeping them facedown. Now, take the two piles and put them one on top of the other. Be careful not to mix up the cards.

3. Now tell everyone you can identify the two cards your friend picked out. (If they doubt you, scoff at their ignorance.) Search through the deck and pull out the two cards that are different colors from the surrounding cards. Amazing!

THE SMALLEST

Bigger isn't necessarily better. Want proof? Have a look at these cool things in really small packages.

...HORSE

In 2006, *Guinness World Records* officially named Thumbelina—a 17½-inch-tall horse from Missouri—the world's smallest. She weighed only 8½ pounds when she was born (about the size of a human newborn) and today is so small that she sleeps with the family's dogs...in their doghouse.

...FROG

When they're fully grown, Gardiner's Seychelles frogs are only about half an inch long. And newly hatched babies are just a tenth of an inch long. These tiny amphibians live on the Seychelles, a chain of islands in the Indian Ocean, and they come out mostly at night to hunt for food. Their favorite prey? Mites—microscopic insects that live in soil and water.

...HUMAN WAIST

Cathie Jung from Connecticut has the world's smallest waist. It's only 15 inches—about as big as most people's necks. How did she get it that small? By using a type of underwear called a corset. Jung thought tiny waists looked attractive, so she spent 25 years lacing her corsets tighter...and tighter. In fact, except when she's in the shower, she's never without a corset. It's a tough life, though. She can't really bend over. "I find it tricky sitting in low chairs," she says. "Sometimes, I have to sit in the high chair."

...HUMANOID ROBOT

At just over six inches tall, this toy robot dances and even plays air guitar. The i-SOBOT from Japan is the smallest human-shaped robot in the world. It comes in a variety of colors (blue and white are the most popular). But it doesn't come cheap—bringing one of these home will cost about $230.

...GUITAR

In 2003, researchers at Cornell University in New York built two nanoguitars. They're so small—about the size of one human cell—that you can see them only through a microscope. But the scientists insist that not only are the guitars really there, their six strings (each is 100 atoms wide) are playable, too...even if the volume is so low no one can hear it.

* * *

WORLD'S LONGEST NOSE

Every year, Turkey holds a "world's longest nose" contest to see who's got the biggest snout. Since 2005, a man named Mehmet Ozyure—and his 3½-inch-long nose—have held the title. (On average, a human nose is about 2 inches long.)

DIM STARS

Why do we listen to celebrities?

"Smoking kills. If you're killed, you've lost a very important part of your life."
—**Brooke Shields**

"I have opinions of my own—strong opinions— but I don't always agree with them."
—**George W. Bush**

"Fiction writing is great. You can make up almost anything."
—**Ivana Trump**

"If we don't succeed, we run the risk of failure."
—**Dan Quayle, former vice president**

"Whenever I watch TV and see those poor starving kids all over the world, I can't help but cry. I mean I'd love to be skinny like that but not with all those flies and death and stuff."
—**Mariah Carey**

"These people haven't seen the last of my face. If I go down, I'm going down standing up."
—**Chuck Person, basketball player**

"So, where's the Cannes Film Festival being held this year?"
—**Christina Aguilera**

"It was God who made me so beautiful. If I weren't, then I'd be a schoolteacher."
—**Linda Evangelista, supermodel**

BRIGHT STARS

Oh, maybe this is why.

"I don't know the key to success, but the key to failure is trying to please everybody."

—**Bill Cosby**

"My mom is always telling me it takes a long time to get to the top, but a short time to get to the bottom."

—**Miley Cyrus**

"Focusing your life solely on making a buck shows a certain poverty of ambition. It asks too little of yourself. Because it's only when you hitch your wagon to something larger than yourself that you realize your true potential."

—**Barack Obama**

"Always have a vivid imagination, for you never know when you might need it."

—**J. K. Rowling**

"Dealing with backstabbers, there was one thing I learned. They're only powerful when you've got your back turned."

—**Eminem**

"I'm only young once. Who cares if I'm a goofball?

—**Ashton Kutcher**

"My grandmother once told me, 'Don't let failure go to your heart and don't let success go to your head.'"

—**Will Smith**

THE HOUSE THAT SARAH BUILT

Sarah Winchester was incredibly wealthy...and incredibly wacky. She spent more than 30 years building a house that (she hoped) would keep her safe from evil spirits.

LOADED!

Sarah Pardee married William Winchester in 1862. She was the daughter of a wealthy Connecticut family, and he was the son of Oliver Winchester, owner of the Winchester rifle company. In 1860, the company had developed the first rifle that could fire a series of bullets without reloading. (Before that, you had to clean and reload the gun after each bullet was fired.) Sales of that rifle—and many more that followed—earned the Winchester family millions of dollars.

MILLION-HEIRESS

Life was hard for Sarah. Her infant daughter died in 1866, and she never had another child. Then, in 1880, her father-in-law died, and her husband caught tuberculosis. He passed away the following year.

All of that was terrible, but it made Sarah extremely rich. She inherited $20 million and about half of the Winchester company, which brought her an additional $1,000 every day.

CURSED!

Soon after the death of her husband, Sarah started visiting psychics for comfort. One of them told her that the Winchesters had been cursed by the spirits of all the people who had been killed by their guns. According to that psychic, these spirits demanded revenge and were after Sarah. What's more, her dead husband wanted her to move out of New England to escape the family curse. But there was a catch—once she started building a new home, she must never stop...not even for one hour. If she did, the evil spirits would claim her just as they had her baby, her father-in-law, and her husband.

Terrified, Sarah sold her home in Connecticut and moved to California. She found property in San Jose, not far from San Francisco. In 1884, she began building a house—construction went on nonstop for 36 years.

IF SHE BUILDS IT...

Sarah started with a farmhouse that sat on more than 160 acres, and she hired a team of carpenters to work on it around the clock. Every night at midnight, she held a séance to summon "good" spirits who, she said, provided the next day's building plans.

There were no master plans—the carpenters just kept expanding the house. Rooms were built around rooms and doors opened to walls.

By 1906, the house stood seven stories high. Then on April 18, a strong earthquake struck, and the top three floors collapsed,

---

Tears are made of almost all the same ingredients as urine.

trapping Sarah in a bedroom. She was eventually freed, but believed that the incident was the spirits' way of telling her they were unhappy with her home improvements. To appease them, she boarded up 30 rooms in the front of the house.

But because the original psychic had said construction couldn't stop, Sarah kept building. This time, though, she had a plan...sort of. She installed secret rooms, trapdoors, upside-down stair posts, and chimneys that didn't work—all in an attempt to confuse the evil spirits that were after her.

HOW MYSTERIOUS

The hammering, sawing, and construction commotion came to a sudden stop on September 5, 1922, when 83-year-old Sarah Winchester died in her sleep. When told of her death, the workmen quit what they were doing immediately. Some even left half-pounded nails in the walls.

Today, the home, called the Winchester Mystery House, is open for tours. There are 160 rooms, 950 doors, 367 steps, 47 fireplaces, 17 chimneys, 3 elevators, and 2 basements. Spiderwebs and the number 13 show up everywhere: there are 13 candle holders in the chandelier and 13 stones in the spider-web-patterned stained-glass window. And the house is supposed to be haunted. Visitors claim to have heard mysterious footsteps, banging doors, and even Sarah herself playing the piano. So if you do visit, keep an eye out for ghosts.

YOU ARE SO ANNOYING!

*How come some of the most popular movies
have the most annoying characters?*

SEND HIM FAR, FAR AWAY
Star Wars Episode I: The Phantom Menace
is one of the highest-grossing American
movies of all time. Millions of people saw the
film, and it seems like almost of all of them were
annoyed by the character of Jar Jar Binks. Even 10 years
after the movie was released, he still ranks first on audience polls of the most annoying movie characters of all
time.

A surprising twist: George Lucas, the creator of the
Star Wars movies, didn't intend for Jar Jar to be annoying. He was supposed to be funny so that he'd appeal to
kids. The Star Wars team spent more than a year devel-
oping how Jar Jar looked, how he talked, how he moved.
He's tall and gangly, and he has a face that looks like a
floppy-eared duck-billed platypus with stringy growths
that resemble dreadlocks coming out of his head. The
thing that most annoyed audiences, though, was Jar Jar's
voice. He had a dopey way of speaking that many people
found irritating. (So if you *really* want to annoy your
teacher, start talking like Jar Jar.)

Lucas and his team were surprised that people had

The kea of New Zealand is the world's only mountain-dwelling parrot.

such a negative reaction to Jar Jar. But they listened to the audience and cut back his role for the next film, *Star Wars Episode II: Attack of the Clones*.

ALWAYS ANNOYING, BUT ALWAYS FUNNY

Besides being incredibly annoying, Ace in *Ace Ventura: Pet Detective*, Stanley Ipkiss in *The Mask*, and Lloyd Christmas in *Dumb and Dumber* all have something in common: they were played by Jim Carrey. Ace Ventura was Jim Carrey's first big starring role, and since that movie came out in 1994, Carrey has had a successful career playing annoying characters.

According to many movie buffs, the things that some people find annoying about Jim Carrey's characters are what others think are funny: his goofy faces, silly voices, and gross jokes. People even repeat his catchphrases—like Ace Ventura's "All-righty then."

Movie reviewers used words like "stupid," "gross," and "immature" to describe all three movies, but they were all hits and made Jim Carrey a superstar.

* * *

SPF Goo: Hippos ooze a red liquid from their skin's pores. The ancient Greeks saw it and believed hippos sweated blood when they got too hot. But the Greeks were wrong—the red liquid is a natural sunscreen.

WALK ON WATER

Why swim or take a boat across the ocean when
you can walk like Rémy Bricka did?

O## NE-MAN OPERATION
In the early 1900s, one-man bands—in which a person strapped a bunch of instruments to his body and played them all at once—were popular. But by the 1980s, few people had heard of them. Still, Rémy Bricka tried anyway, traveling around France as *L'Homme Orchestre*, or "the One-Man Band." Not many people turned out to see his act, so Bricka decided he needed to find another way to drum up some publicity. That's when he came up with the idea of crossing the Atlantic Ocean...on foot.

Obviously, he couldn't use regular shoes, so Bricka made two 14-foot-long miniature boats—a combination of canoes, water skis, and shoes made out of fiberglass—and strapped them to his feet. To propel himself across the water (and help him balance), he built a six-foot-long, double-bladed paddle.

STAYIN' ALIVE

Bricka estimated that he'd be alone on the ocean for at least two months, so he knew he needed to take care of his basic needs. He planned to tow a small boat behind him, containing a sleeping chamber (it was actually a coffin without a lid), navigation devices, some food, and three water-purifying machines to make the salty seawater drinkable. He also packed his flute, which he would play to calm his nerves during any storms he encountered.

SEA CRUISE

On April 2, 1988, Bricka set out from the Canary Islands, off the northern coast of Africa. His destination: the Caribbean island of Guadeloupe, about 3,500 miles away. He wanted to make the trip in 60 days, which meant he'd have to "walk" more than 50 miles a day in his fiberglass boat shoes.

Standing upright, rowing and towing his small boat, Bricka made good time. He glided across the water like a skier does on snow, and also tied a kite to his back that harnessed the power of the wind to move him forward. As fish and plankton swam or drifted by, Bricka scooped them up and ate them raw.

January 16—National Nothing Day—was first observed (or not) in 1973.

SOMETHING'S FISHY

Still, the trip wasn't easy. Two of the three water desalinators broke, and the remaining one couldn't purify enough water to meet his needs. So Bricka drank a quart of seawater each day—a dangerous decision that can lead to severe dehydration. He had also underestimated the amount of fish he'd be able to catch, and most days, he didn't get enough to eat. His weight dropped from 160 pounds to 110 pounds.

But he kept going, and on May 31, 1988, he finally made it. A Japanese boat picked him up off the coast of Trinidad—an island about 300 miles south of his intended destination of Guadeloupe. This meant Bricka had actually walked across more ocean than he'd meant to.

TOUGH ACT TO FOLLOW

Rémy Bricka had successfully "walked" across 3,502 miles of ocean in just 60 days, a feat that earned him a spot in *Guinness World Records*. He recovered fully and returned to France, where—thanks to his new celebrity status—his one-man band act drew larger crowds for the next few months.

More than 10 years went by, and nobody dared to try to beat his astounding accomplishment until Bricka decided to do it himself. In April 2000, he set out to cross the Pacific Ocean on his fiberglass boat shoes. He left Los Angeles, hoping to arrive in Sydney, Australia, five months later, just in time for the Summer

Olympics. This trip would be a lot harder—the Pacific Ocean is much bigger than the Atlantic. The distance from Los Angeles to Sydney: 7,500 miles.

COMING UP SHORT

This time, though, Bricka was better prepared. His boat carried $100,000 worth of equipment, including a satellite phone, a GPS tracking device, and freeze-dried meals. He got a corporate sponsor—Stoeffler, a French food supplier—to pay for it all. The company even donated an 11-pound tub of sauerkraut.

But once again, nothing went smoothly. In August, his phone broke, and he ran out of food (including the sauerkraut). Then a storm blew in, causing 50-foot swells that roughed up him and his boat. Fortunately, he had a backup handheld text messaging device. So Bricka wrote to his wife back in Paris: "Come pick me up now, or I'll have to hitchhike."

Ten days later, an American tuna boat found him 500 miles south of Hawaii. He'd been out 153 days and covered 4,847 miles. He hadn't made it all the way to Australia, but it was still a longer journey than his Atlantic Ocean trip.

So what motivates someone to walk across the ocean? "Our time on Earth goes by very quickly," Bricka says. "In eternity, our time is one second. So in this second, I will use this time to realize my dream."

THE KING'S MENU

Elvis Presley made great music, but his food preferences were a little odd. Imagine what your teachers would say if you showed up with these snacks.

ROYAL ROADKILL
Young Elvis's family was so poor that they often ate squirrels, possums, pigs' feet, and pigs' ears for dinner.

HIS FAVORITE FOODS
- Fried peanut butter and banana sandwiches
- Burned bacon
- Sauerkraut
- Chitterlings (boiled animal intestines)

FANTASTIC FOOD FEAT
When he was in his 20s, Elvis could eat eight cheeseburgers and two BLTs, and drink three milk shakes...all in one sitting!

WHAT WOULD YOU DO FOR A PB&J?
Elvis once flew to Denver, Colorado, after hearing about a restaurant that made great peanut butter and jelly sandwiches. He had 22 of them delivered to the airport runway and ate them on the flight back to Memphis.

During his lifetime, Elvis Presley gave away more than 80 Cadillacs.

25 WAYS TO SPELL SHAXBERD

*The next time you get marked down on an assignment
for poor spelling, consider telling your teacher that
you spell words "the Elizabethan way."*

THE NAME GAME

Almost everyone considers William Shakespeare to be the greatest writer in the history of the English language. His plays—like *Hamlet*, *Romeo and Juliet*, *Macbeth*, and *A Midsummer Night's Dream*—are widely performed today. And in his own time (the late 1500s and early 1600s), his plays were the most popular in London. But as much as everyone loved Shakespeare in those days, there was one thing they had trouble agreeing on: how to spell his name.

In Shakespeare's era (called the "Elizabethan era," because Queen Elizabeth I was the queen of England at the time), the spelling of words was often inexact. Back then, very few people could read, and Londoners spoke in many different dialects. That made spelling a tricky business. The result: historians have discovered that "Shakespeare" was spelled at least 25 different ways from the time he was born in 1564 to 1623, when his plays were first published.

WILLIAM WHO?

His name was always pronounced the same, and the differences in spelling had to do with the different ways people wrote the same sounds. For example, "ck," "ks," "kes," and "x" all made the same sound, and in some accents, "berd" could even sound like "peare." Why? In Shakespeare's day, there was no authority on how to spell words, and no common dictionary to look them up in, so spellings always varied.

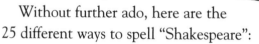

    Without further ado, here are the 25 different ways to spell "Shakespeare":

1) The most common spelling was "Shakespeare."
2) Shakespere
3) Shakespear
4) Shakspeare
5) Shackspeare
6) Shakspere
7) Shackespeare
8) Shackspere
9) Shackespere
10) Shaxpere
11) Shexpere
12) Shakspe-
13) Shake-speare
14) Shaxberd
15) Shak-speare
16) Shakspear
17) Shagspere
18) Shaksper
19) Shaxpeare
20) Shaxper
21) Shakespe
22) Shakp
23) Shaksp.
24) Shakespheare
25) Shakspe

WRONG FACTS

In 1492, Columbus sailed the ocean blue…
well, at least that much is true.

FACT? *Italian Christopher Columbus sailed under the flag of Spain because he couldn't get financial backing at home for his voyages. Everybody thought the world was flat and worried that he would sail off the edge.*
WRONG! Columbus wanted to sail west to Asia. Everybody else had sailed east, but Columbus thought a trip west would be faster and easier. He did have a hard time getting money for the trip, but it wasn't because people in the 1400s thought the world was flat. Educated people knew the world was round. Investors and the Italian government thought Columbus was underestimating how far away Asia was. They didn't want to fund his voyage because they thought he'd run out of supplies during the trip.

FACT? *Christopher Columbus discovered America.*
WRONG! He was looking for India, but he actually landed in the Bahamas, not what's technically North America. And he was definitely not the first person to "find" the Americas. Native American tribes had lived there for thousands of years, and Icelandic explorer Leif Eriksson established a colony in Newfoundland (now part of Canada) around AD 1000.

Q: What should you say to a vampire who wins an award? A: "Con-dracula-tions!"

ANOTHER REAL TREASURE HUNT

On page 50, we told you about the gold hidden somewhere in the British Virgin Islands. Here's another hunt. Arrgh…do you have your pirate ship ready?

SEEKING: More than 50 tons of gems, pearls, gold, coins, and silver bars worth around $50 million today.

LAST SEEN…80 to 90 miles north of the Dominican Republic, in an area of the Atlantic Ocean known as the Silver Bank. The place got its name because so many treasure ships sank there.

THE LEGEND: In 1641, the *Nuestra Señora de la Concepción* was loaded with treasure and headed back to Spain from Mexico when a hurricane struck. The ship lost its masts, flooded with water, and then drifted for a week before it smashed into a reef. Most of the crew was killed in the wreck. Soon after, pirates came and stole many of the riches from the disabled ship. But they didn't get far before they hit a nearby reef and went under, too.

The average human bladder can hold two cups of urine for up to five hours. (Yuck!)

Forty-six years after the *Concepción* sank, the British government sent a man named William Phips to find it. In 1687, Phips and his crew started to search hundreds of miles of reef in the Atlantic. Finally, one of his men swam down to admire a coral formation and saw guns—a shipwreck! Another look revealed a chunk of silver.

In all, the Phips crew salvaged 32 tons of treasure—in the process, they had to fight off pirates and other treasure seekers. After a few weeks, though, they ran out of food and water and had to leave the *Concepción* behind.

KEEP LOOKING

Phips kept only a sixteenth of the riches he found—he turned the rest over to England. King James II eventually made him a knight and the governor of the Massachusetts colony. But he never recovered the remaining *Concepción* loot.

Three hundred years later, another American tried. In 1978, a treasure hunter named Burt Webber found Phips's site. Amazingly, some treasure remained, including 60,000 silver coins, gold bullion, and expensive Chinese porcelain. Even though the shipwreck had been plundered many times over the years, the *Concepción's* leftovers were still worth $14 million!

Want another treasure tale? Sail over to page 220 to read about Blackbeard and his lost loot.

TO THE NINES

In honor of page 99, here are some lists of 9s.

9 WORDS FOR "FART"

Onara (Japanese)

Pête (French)

Pongu (Korean)

Pedo (Spanish)

Pierdziec (Polish)

Furz (German)

Szellentés (Hungarian)

Fasia (Arabic)

Todt (Thai)

9 HIGHEST-GROSSING MOVIES

Titanic

The Dark Knight

Star Wars: A New Hope

Shrek 2

E.T.: The Extra-Terrestrial

Phantom Menace

Pirates of the Caribbean 2

Spider-Man

Revenge of the Sith

9 LARGEST CITIES IN THE WORLD

Tokyo, Japan

Seoul, South Korea

Mexico City

New York City

Mumbai, India

Jakarta, Indonesia

São Paulo, Brazil

Delhi, India

Osaka, Japan

9 DEADLIEST SNAKES

Inland Taipan

King Brown Snake

Malayan Krait

Coastal Taipan

Tiger Snake

Beaked Sea Snake

Saw-Scaled Viper

Coral Snake

Death Adder

9 FASTEST ANIMALS

Cheetah (70 mph)

Antelope (61 mph)

Wildebeest (50 mph)

Lion (50 mph)

Gazelle (50 mph)

Quarter horse (47 mph)

Elk (45 mph)

Cape Hunting Dog (45 mph)

Coyote (43 mph)

9 HIGHEST PAID SPORTS STARS IN 2008

Tiger Woods

Phil Mickelson

LeBron James

Floyd Mayweather

Kobe Bryant

Shaquille O'Neal

Alex Rodriguez

Kevin Garnett

Peyton Manning

Except for royalty, ancient Egyptians didn't bother recording birth dates.

BAD ADVICE

You've been told not to do these things because they're "bad" for you (or others). But as it turns out, they're all perfectly fine.

Don't read in dim light—you'll hurt your eyes.
According to the American Academy of Ophthalmology, good light makes reading easier and limits eye strain, but using poor light "causes no permanent eye damage."

Don't touch a baby bird—its mother will abandon it.
Whether or not a mother can detect the scent of a human depends on the animal's sense of smell. Most birds have a poor sense of smell, and would never be able to tell if a human had touched their nest. (Still, it's best to leave birds' nests alone.)

Don't crack your knuckles—it'll make them bigger and you'll eventually get arthritis.
Go ahead and crack them. It's harmless.

Don't watch TV in the dark—it's bad for your eyes.
This is also a myth. Watching TV in a dark room doesn't cause any eye damage at all. (Brain damage is another matter.) The idea came from an advertising executive in the 1950s named J. Robert Mendte, who spread the fiction in commercials on behalf of one of his clients—a lamp company.

Actual label on a Sears hair dryer: "Do not use while sleeping."

MISCHIEF MAKERS

Didn't do your homework? Blame it on a faun,
Menehune, or another mythological character.

MENEHUNE

According to the Hawaiians, the Menehune are an ancient race of pixies who live in the islands' jungles. The Menehune are usually said to be about two feet tall, but can be as small as six inches. Legend has it that they are wary of humans but like to play tricks on them (like sneaking into houses to hide people's shoes or car keys). And to ensure they're never seen, the Menehune make all their mischief at night. They also love to eat fish and bananas, and enjoy diving from cliffs. Hawaiian parents often tell their children that splashes heard outside at night are just the Menehune having fun.

KAPPA

These are water spirits that supposedly live in lakes and rivers in Japan. They are the size of children, but have froglike bodies, the faces of monkeys, webbed hands and feet, and scaly green skin. On top of their heads is a small depression filled with a liquid that's said to give them their mischievous powers. The kappa like to cause trouble, and Japanese children blame them when something—*anything*—goes wrong. (Did somebody fart? Nope. It was a kappa.)

The kappa are considered devilish creatures, but they're also curious about humans. So if you happen to see a kappa, you're supposed to do one of two things:

- Bow to him. The kappa will have to return your bow (it's only polite) and, in doing so, will spill the liquid from its head. That will make him weak, and he'll have to go back to his watery home.

- Befriend him by offering a cucumber (the kappa's favorite food). Once a kappa is your pal, he can be very useful. Legend says the kappa taught the Japanese how to water their crops and how to set broken bones.

FAUNS

Ancient Romans believed in genies, ancestral spirits who kept watch over different places. The genies of forests and woodlands were called fauns. From the waist down, fauns were goats, with hooves and fur; from the waist up, they were human, but had goatlike horns and whiskers. Fauns liked to play music and play games in the woods. Humans, however, were their enemy, and to protect their forests, fauns would do just about anything...including kidnapping children who wandered too far into the forest. (So be careful not to wander too far into any ancient Roman forests.)

NUTS!

Uncle John loves peanut butter and prefers his PB&JB (peanut butter and jelly bean) sandwiches toasted. Quick— read this story before he finishes the last bite!

PASTY PEANUTS

People have been eating peanuts for thousands of years, but peanut butter is a fairly recent development. It didn't appear until the late 1800s, and no one knows who deserves credit for its invention. That's because two men in different states both came up with an idea for peanut butter around the same time.

In 1890, a doctor (his name has been lost to history) from St. Louis, Missouri, talked a local food manufacturer into making a ground peanut paste. He thought it would be a great source of protein for patients who had lost their teeth and couldn't chew meat. About the same time, another doctor (this one was from Michigan) did something similar because he worried that his vegetarian patients weren't getting enough protein.

The second doctor was John Harvey Kellogg. He never did much with the peanut butter. Instead, he went on to make a fortune in cereal. But one of his employees, Joseph Lambert, took the idea and turned it into a success. Soon he was selling hand-operated grinders to make peanut paste, and in 1899, his wife published a book that included one of the first recipes for peanut butter.

IT'S GOTTA BE SMOOOTH

Early peanut butter didn't taste very good. That's because Lambert used boiled peanuts (not very flavorful) instead of roasted. It was also gritty because the grinders couldn't completely smooth out all of the tiny peanut pieces and left behind grainy bits.

In 1904, that all changed when a man named C. H. Sumner introduced peanut butter made from roasted peanuts at the St. Louis World's Fair. Sumner sold more than $700 worth of his peanut butter at the fair—more than most people at that time made in an entire year.

Then, in 1922, a Californian figured out how to stir the peanut paste until it was creamy. The first company to buy the technology: E. K. Pond, which in 1928 renamed itself Peter Pan. By the 1950s, brands like Jif and Skippy had also been created, and peanut butter had become a staple in American diets. Today, people in the United States buy a jar of peanut butter every three seconds, about 90 million jars each year.

BRAINTEASERS

Can you figure out these twisty, turny word puzzles?
(Answers are on page 241.)

1.
MILL1ION

2.
PANTS
PANTS

3.

   L
 I L
B   y

4.
 R
ROADS
A
D
S

5.
T _ R N

6.
D   H
 E T
  A

7.
 T
 U
 H
 S

8.
hijklmno

9.
STONE

10.
 R
 O
RAIL
 D

11.
T
O
U
C
H

12.
VISION
VISION

13.
VA DERS

14.
CLOUD
TH

15.
STEP
SPETS
SPETS

READY, SET, FLY!

People have been imagining themselves as paper pilots ever since the first trees were pressed into paper. Here is how to make a simple, classic paper airplane.

1. Start with a piece of rectangular paper. Photocopier paper seems to work best...but your old homework may work, too.

2. Fold the paper neatly in half, lengthwise. Open it up again, and lay it flat.

3. Fold each of the top two corners in to meet the center crease.

4. Now you'll narrow the plane by folding in the edges at the top to meet the center crease. Keep the point sharp, and make sure the creases are neat.

5. Fold the plane in half lengthwise so it looks like a triangle.

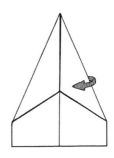

The ancient Chinese called eggplants "mad apples," believing they caused insanity.

6. Fold down one top edge to create a wing. Repeat on the other side.

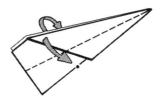

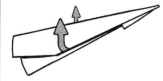

7. Hold the paper horizontally and open the wings so they stick out flat on either side.

8. Hold the body of the plane and give it a gentle toss. Now you're flying!

DID YOU KNOW?

- A paper airplane flies because your throw gives it power. It speeds up because of kinetic energy—that's the energy or force an object gets as it accelerates. After that, your airplane's wings keep it airborne by pushing the air around them backward and down. This is a lot like what makes a real airplane fly.

- In space, because there's no air for it to navigate through, a paper airplane would just float in a straight line until it ran into something.

- Longest paper airplane flight: 27.6 seconds.

- Longest distance: 193 feet.

- Largest paper airplane wingspan: 40 feet, 10 inches.

CRAZY CONTESTS

Tired of watching your dog chase his tail?
Then check out these beastly games.

BEETLE WRESTLE MANIA
Rhinoceros beetles are huge insects. They can grow to be up to six inches long and have a tough outer shell and horns. And for their size, they are the strongest animals on earth—they can lift more than 850 times their own weight. (An elephant can lift only about 25 percent of its body weight.) They're popular pets in Japan, so to give the beetles a workout (and have some fun in the process), kids enter their big bugs in local tournaments. The rules go like this: two rhino beetles fight each other in a 20-inch-wide ring, and one emerges victorious when he throws his competitor out of the ring...or the competitor walks out by himself.

WHAT A LOVELY CAMEL YOU HAVE

People say beauty is in the eye of the beholder, and that's definitely true in the United Arab Emirates (UAE). Every spring, camel breeders from all over the Middle East bring their beasts to the UAE's capital city of Abu Dhabi to compete in a...beauty contest. Camels have been an important part of Middle Eastern culture for thousands of years because they're perfectly suited for life in the desert. They can go for months without drinking water, can carry heavy loads, and are a source of milk and meat. So as a way to honor them, the UAE's government organized the first Abu Dhabi Camel Festival in 2002. Today, more than 10,000 camels compete each year to win a variety of prizes— about $9 million and 100 new cars. One judge says, "It's just like judging a beautiful girl. You look for big eyes, long lashes, and a long neck—maybe 39 or 40 inches."

...which he frequently misplaced.

SCHOOLS OF THE AIR

If you lived in the Australian Outback between 1950 and 2005, you might have gone to school on the radio.

OUTBACK SCHOOL
In Australia, most of the people live along the coast. That's because the country's interior is mostly open desert and rocky rangeland. Only about 10 percent of Australia's entire population lives in the dusty interior, which is known as the Outback.

The folks who do live there mostly work on sheep or cattle ranches. Their nearest neighbors can be 100 miles away, and roads are rutted dirt. It's so isolated that, until 1950, kids who grew up in the Outback had to attend boarding school if they wanted to get an education—there weren't enough people living out there to build schools. But in 1950, a woman named Adelaide Miethke came up with the idea of using airplanes and radios to link kids throughout the Outback with teachers in large towns.

THANK THE FLYING DOCTORS

In 1928, the Australian government set up an airplane ambulance service for people living in the Outback. Each home had a two-way radio that people could use to call for help in case of an emergency. A doctor would fly in on a small plane and either treat the victim right there or take him to a hospital in one of the cities. It was called the Royal Flying Doctor Service.

Adelaide Miethke worked for the service, and she began to wonder why the government couldn't use the same technology to set up schools for kids living on the ranches. It took a few tries, but she presented a plan to the government, and in 1950, the first school opened in a town called Alice Springs. It was called the School of the Air.

HOW IT WORKED

Each teacher for the school had a small office in one of the Outback towns. The students sat in their own houses hundreds of miles away next to their radios. In the school's early days, the teacher just presented a 3½-hour lesson and the kids listened—they had no way to talk to her. But eventually, the school got two-way radios and the kids could talk to the teacher and to each other.

At least once a year, teachers went on "patrol." That meant they drove to each child's home (no matter how far away it was) to meet the kids face-to-face and talk to their parents. The rest of the year, airplanes for the Royal Flying Doctor Service delivered mail, homework, and supplies to teachers and students.

No one's sure: Wilma Flintstone's maiden name was either Pebble or Slaghoopal.

OUTBACK SCHOOL TODAY

Alice Springs was just the first School of the Air. In all, 15 schools opened throughout the Australian Outback. Today, they're a little different but serve basically the same needs. Kids stopped using radios in 2005, and they no longer send in their homework by airplane. Now they use e-mail and Web cams to communicate with their teachers. But teachers still do "patrol" visits, and today, about 1,000 students are enrolled in the program. Without the Schools of the Air, those kids would have to leave their families to get an education, or they might not be able to go to school at all.

MYTH-CONCEPTIONS

A lot of the things you may have been told just aren't true.

Myth: Monkeys and apes groom each other by picking off fleas and ticks, and then they eat them.
Truth: They're not removing bugs, they're removing dead skin. (But they do eat it.)

Myth: Ninjas wore all black.
Truth: When movies and TV shows started showing ninjas—secret agents in old Japan—they borrowed the details from 19th-century Japanese plays, which put ninjas in black clothing because it looked mysterious and dramatic onstage. In reality, ninjas wore dark blue at night to fade into the dark. During the day, they wore whatever clothes they needed to blend in with crowds.

Myth: Diamonds are the world's most valuable gems.
Truth: Carat for carat (the measurement used to weigh gems), rubies are more valuable than diamonds.

Myth: An arm or limb "falls asleep" because its blood supply gets cut off.
Truth: The feeling of numbness happens when a major

Popular snack in Uganda: *Nsenene*—green grasshoppers fried in oil, with salt.

nerve is pinched against a hard object or bone. The pinch causes a temporary numb sensation, but the blood continues to flow normally.

Myth: The Eskimo language has hundreds of different words for "snow."
Truth: There is no single group of people called "Eskimos," so there is no one "Eskimo language." The term refers to dozens of different ethnic groups in northern North America, most of whom speak their own language. Each has its own word for "snow."

Myth: Chameleons change color to blend into their environment.
Truth: Chameleons can change color, but it's a reaction to fear, extreme temperature, or light changes. And different chameleons turn different colors; it does help them survive. But the change has nothing to do with matching their surroundings.

Myth: In the original fairy tale, Cinderella's slippers were made of glass.
Truth: Actually, they were made of fur. The goof comes from a poor translation—someone interpreted the French word *vair*, which means "fox fur," as *verre*, which means "glass."

SWEAT 101

Everything you ever needed to know about sweat.

- People sweat to cool themselves off. As the sweat evaporates from your skin, it lowers your body's temperature.

- On a hot summer day, most people sweat about three cups per hour.

- Ninety-nine percent of sweat is water; the rest is mostly potassium and salt

- Who sweats more—Olympic athletes or football players? Probably the Olympians, especially if they're playing a sport that requires constant activity, like tennis or soccer. Competitors in men's tennis produce about 14 cups of sweat per match. That beats the football players—even on a very hot day, they usually sweat less than five cups per game.

- Sweat stinks, right? Nope. It's odorless. The bacteria that thrive in it are what smell.

- The human body contains as many as 4 million sweat glands. Your feet have the most, and your back has the least.

- Women have more sweat glands than men, but men's glands are more active, which is why it often seems like men sweat more than women.

- Despite what many people think, dogs do have sweat

glands, mostly on their paws. But they have far fewer than humans, so they also pant to cool themselves off.

- Two things cause your body to sweat: high heat and stress. Why? Stress makes your body think it's under attack, so it produces a chemical called adrenaline to give you extra strength to fight back or run away. All that activity would raise your body's temperature, so you sweat in anticipation of it. That worked well for our ancestors, who had to fight off wild animals and other real attacks. But in modern times, sweating is just a leftover evolutionary reaction...that usually stresses people out even more.

DUMB CROOKS

For these guys, crime really didn't pay.

BUMP

Oops: In January 2009, 20-year-old Santiago Alonso was driving down a Massachusetts street when he hit another car. Frightened that he'd get in trouble, he immediately drove away. The problem? His car's bumper had fallen off during the accident. Just a bumper wouldn't have been so bad...but it also had the car's license plate attached to it.

Gotcha! The police easily tracked Alonso down and arrested him for making an unsafe lane change and for fleeing the scene of an accident.

NO KIDDING

Oops: When Barry Kramer decided to rob a sporting-goods store in Utah in November 2008, he realized he needed a weapon and a disguise. What did he choose? A 10-inch butcher knife and a pair of men's underwear. He walked into the store with the underwear on his head and demanded that the clerk give him all the cash in the register. According to police reports, the clerk first said, "You've gotta be kidding me!" and then tried to wrestle the knife away from Kramer. The blade broke, so Kramer ran.

Gotcha! Outside the store, two customers tackled Kramer and sat on him until the police arrived.

BEATING THE GROWN-UPS

These amazing young athletes took to the field
against some of the world's best...and won!

FREDDY ADU

This future soccer star immigrated to the United States from the African nation of Ghana in 1997, when he was eight. By then, Freddy had already been playing soccer for more than five years and was used to going up against much older players in his hometown. So when a coach in his Maryland neighborhood saw him play and asked him to join a team of boys a few years older than he was, Freddy signed up right away.

In 2003, Freddy became an American citizen, and the next year, a few months before he turned 15, he made his professional debut as a forward and midfielder for the D.C. United. He played with and scored goals against men several years older, and he was the youngest American athlete to join a professional team in more than 100 years. Freddy was also a star student: he got his high-school diploma when he was 15 years old, just a few months after becoming a Major League soccer player.

MARIA SHARAPOVA

In 1991, at the age of four, Maria started playing tennis in her hometown of Nya-gan, Russia. By six, she was so good that she'd impressed the head coach of the Russian Tennis Federation. By seven, she'd moved to the United States to train at the Bollettieri Sports Acade-my in Bradenton, Florida, a school that had produced tennis stars like Andre Agassi and Monica Seles. At first, her father had to work several jobs to pay for her training. But just a few months after she got to Florida, Maria was such a tennis talent that she won a full scholarship to the academy.

For the next seven years, Maria competed in amateur matches, placing first in so many of them that she won tennis's first "Rising Star Award." In 2001, when she turned 14, she went pro and became the youngest per-son to reach the final at the Australian Open's junior division. But her biggest success came in 2004, when she headed to Wimbledon. She made it all the way to the final (which no one expected the 17-year-old to do) and had to face Serena Williams, one of the best players in the world. But thanks to 100-mph serves and quick feet, Maria won the match—becoming the first Russian and the third-youngest person ever to win Wimbledon. (The two younger winners were Lottie Dodd, age 15, in 1887, and Martina Hingis, age 16, in 1997.)

RYAN SHECKLER

This California kid started riding a skateboard when he was 18 months old. He wasn't doing tricks back then, but he loved scooting around his driveway on one knee. By 1996, when he was just seven, Ryan had landed his first commercial sponsor (a local skate shop) and was winning amateur skateboarding contests. Then in 2003, he went pro...and at 13 won a gold medal at the Summer X Games, becoming the youngest person ever to do so. He's taken first place in more than 15 professional competitions since, and even has his own MTV reality show, *Life of Ryan*. When a reporter asked him if he knew he'd be this successful, Ryan said, "I always thought it would happen, just not so soon!"

* * *

WHY DOES ORANGE JUICE TASTE SO BAD AFTER I BRUSH MY TEETH?

Scientists aren't sure, but they think it has to do with a chemical reaction that occurs when you put both things in your mouth. Sodium lauryl sulfate makes toothpaste sudsy, but it also suppresses your taste buds' sweet receptors. Orange juice is contains both sweet and bitter flavors. So if you drink orange juice but have no working sweet receptors, all you taste is the bitter part.

The *Peanuts* comic strip was originally called *Li'l Folks*.

SMELLY SCIENCE

P-U! These facts sure do stink!

- Every person has a unique scent (the same way that everyone has a unique set of fingerprints). The exception: identical twins. They smell exactly the same—minus the perfume, soap, and shampoo, of course.

- On average, girls have a sharper sense of smell than boys do.

- Humans can discern between more than 10,000 different odors. Most of these pass in and out of your nose without your noticing. It's only when a smell is particularly good or bad that your brain pays attention.

- Your sense of smell gets better throughout the day, and is sharpest in the evening.

- Some people have no sense of smell, a condition called anosmia.

- About 80 percent of taste is actually smell. That's why food tastes so bland when you have a stuffy nose.

- People remember facts better when they attach a smell to the fact and then re-create the smell when they need to remember. So next time you've got a test, try using a certain soap when you study. Then use the same soap on test day. You should have an easier time remembering the answers.

THE TRUTH ABOUT SEA MONSTERS

Lurking in the ocean is an enormous sea monster that, according to myth, likes to eat fishing boats and fishermen. Is it just a legend…or is it real?

SEA TALES

Sailors have been telling stories about tentacled sea monsters for thousands of years. Paintings from ancient Greece show giant animals attacking fishing boats. In Norway, sailors feared the mythological kraken, a vicious sea creature with long arms and enormous eyes. But it wasn't until the late 19th century that someone actually brought home hard evidence of one of these "monsters."

HAUL IT IN!

In 1873, a man and his son were fishing off the coast of Newfoundland, Canada, when they saw something that appeared to be a huge squid floating in the water. When the curious fisherman poked the animal, it reared up, wrapped its tentacles around their small boat, and tried to eat it. But the boy took a hatchet, chopped off one of the tentacles, and the creature slithered back into the sea. The pair collected the tentacle (which was about 19 feet long) and brought it back to shore.

A year or so later, the tentacle—and a complete body of a similar creature that had washed up on the shore of Newfoundland—made their way to a Yale University professor named Addison E. Verrill. He did numerous tests on the animal and finally named the sea monster that sailors had been talking about for centuries: he called it the giant squid.

BODY BASICS

Including its head, body, and tentacles, the average giant squid grows to be between 30 and 40 feet long and weighs several hundred pounds. Females, which are bigger than males, can grow to be 600 pounds or more.

The largest giant squid ever found washed up on a New Zealand beach in 1880. It was 65 feet long, including its 40-foot tentacles. How long is that? About the height of a six-story building.

Giant squid also have the largest eyes in the animal kingdom, approximately 10 inches across—the size of dinner plates. These large eyes make it possible for them to see in the deep, dark waters where they live.

HIDE-AND-SEEK

Giant squid are so rare that it wasn't until 2006 that scientists were able to film a live specimen. That year, Japanese researchers filmed a 24-foot female in the ocean about 600 miles off the coast of Tokyo.

NOT THE BIGGEST?

It's hard to imagine, but the giant squid has an even bigger relative: the colossal squid. This creature usually grows to be about the same length as a giant squid, but it's much heavier.

Since 1925, when the first colossal squid was identified, only six others have been found, and all were in the ocean off Antarctica. The largest colossal squid ever captured was in 2007: a 1,091-pounder that was 33 feet long. But it was a male. And since scientists know that female squid are usually bigger than males, they believe there are even larger colossal squid hiding somewhere in the ocean.

*　　*　　*

GIANT SQUID ARE...

- The world's largest cephalopods.
- A sperm whale's main prey.

CHANGE THE NAME!

Even the simplest things in life aren't always what they seem.

- **Poison ivy** isn't poisonous, it's allergenic (it causes allergies). If you come into contact with poison ivy, your skin will start itching and swelling, but touching the plant won't "poison" you. (It's also not even a type of ivy—it's a sumac.)

- Only the day you were born is actually your **birthday**. Each year, you're really celebrating the anniversary of your birth.

- The **Caspian Sea** and the **Dead Sea** aren't seas at all—they're both lakes.

- The **United States of America** is an incorrect term because the nation includes Hawaii. The Pacific islands are not, technically, part of North or South America.

- **Pencil lead** isn't lead—it's a mixture of graphite and clay.

- The **New York Jets** and the **New York Giants** both play their home games in New Jersey.

- **French fries** are not from France. Most likely invented in Belgium, they're called "French" because of the style in which they're sliced (into long, thin strips), known in French as *julienned.*

The turkey didn't come from Turkey—it's native to North America.

ANNOYING JOKES

Uncle John loves a good joke.
He likes these, too.

Q. What does a dog do that a man steps in?
A: Pants

Q. What's at the end of the world?
A. The letter D

Q. What did one mountain say to the other?
A. Do these trees make my butte look fat?

Q. Why was the broom late for work?
A. It over-swept.

Q. Where was the Declaration of Independence signed?
A: At the bottom

Q. Can you spell this sentence without any Rs? "Railroad tracks crisscross."
A. Sure: T-H-I-S S-E-N-T-E-N-C-E

Q. What do you call a boomerang that never comes back?
A: A stick

HA HA

PRESIDENTIAL GOOFS

*To get elected president, you have to
be perfect, right? Not exactly.*

NIXON INSULTS HIS WIFE

Richard Nixon ran for president in 1960
against Senator John F. Kennedy. During the
debates of that campaign—the first ones ever televised—Kennedy came off as handsome and relaxed,
but Nixon sweated profusely and looked nervous.
Then, during their fourth debate, Nixon made a
serious goof. While driving home a point, he declared:
"America can't stand pat!" (To "stand pat" means to
resist change, and Nixon meant that he thought
Kennedy was inflexible.) The trouble was, "Pat" was
also the name of Nixon's wife—and for a minute, many
viewers wondered why he was insisting the country
didn't like her.

Realizing what he'd said, Nixon blushed. He didn't
win the election against Kennedy, but he was eventually
elected president in 1968—with his wife Pat at his side.

GETTING HIS GOAT

Benjamin Harrison, the 23rd president of the United
States (and grandson of William Henry Harrison, the

ninth president), wasn't known as a "people person."
He hated all the socializing that came with being
president. In fact, he was so standoffish and cold that
his staff called him the "Human Iceberg." But Harrison
had a fun side: He liked to skip work in the afternoon
to play with his grandchildren, Mary and Ben, who also
lived in the White House. He bought them a pet goat
that they named His Whiskers.

But the goat was badly behaved, and one day, while
pulling a cart with baby Ben inside it, the goat broke
loose. Trailing the cart behind him, His Whiskers ran
out the White House gate and into the street. President
Harrison saw what happened and took off after them,
waving his walking stick in the air. (Harrison eventually
caught the goat and rescued Ben.)

AHEM, MR. PRESIDENT...

Presidents often entertain heads of state from other countries at state dinners, where good manners are very important. But things don't always go as expected. When President Ronald Reagan hosted François Mitterand, the president of France, and his wife at a White House dinner in 1988, protocol dictated that President Reagan escort Mrs. Mitterand into the dining room.

They walked a few steps together, but then Mrs. Mitterand stopped suddenly. When the president urged her on, she whispered something to him, but he was baffled—he couldn't understand French. Mrs. Mitterand was quietly trying to tell him that she couldn't move because he was standing on the hem of her gown.

*   *   *

IT'S A BLOODY FACT!

- The pressure your heart creates when it pumps your blood is strong enough to squirt it 30 feet.

- Length of the total number of blood vessels in a human body: 60,000 miles...enough to go around the earth 2½ times.

- Lobsters have blue blood.

- The first recorded blood transfusion was performed in England in 1665. It was done between two dogs. The first transfusion on humans was in 1818 (also in England).

A cat has 500 skeletal muscles. (A human has 650.)

DELICIOUS OR DISGUSTING?

Next time you want to bring your teacher a gift, consider one of these foods.

STRANGE FRUIT

The durian from Southeast Asia is one of the largest fruits in the world—about the size of a football—and it's covered in sharp thorns. It can be tricky to harvest: people simply wait for durians to fall off the trees (which grow to be 100 feet tall or more), or use a long pruning saw and gloves to pick them.

And this thorny fruit smells as nasty as it looks. The aroma has been compared to skunk spray, rotting flesh, stale vomit, and sewage. In fact, it smells so bad that many hotels in Southeast Asia won't let tourists take durians into their rooms. They're banned on taxis, buses, ferries, and airplanes, too. There are even "no durian" signs in Singapore's subway stations.

But how does it taste? Surprisingly, most people say it's delicious. If you can get past the stinky exterior, you'll find several sections of cream-colored, custardlike pulp that can be eaten with a spoon. Durians also have large seeds that can be eaten raw, boiled, or roasted. People who love durians pay good money for them—as much as $15 per fruit.

Q. What's a lemniscate? A. It's another name for the infinity sign.

DIRTY, ROTTEN BEANS

Also known as petai beans, "stink beans" are about the size of almonds. They grow in long, thin pods and are used in Thai and Indian food...and are definitely an acquired taste. People who don't like them claim that these crunchy beans smell like a mixture of farts, vomit, rotten garbage, and dirty toilets. But those who love them say that they taste delicious.

LOOK SHARP

If they got lost in the desert, cowboys in the Old West sometimes had to eat cactus plants. And today, people throughout the southwestern United States eat all kinds of cactus dishes—cactus jelly, roasted cactus, fried cactus, even raw cactus.

There are more than 200 species of cacti, and many of them have a sweet, gooey pulp. But beware—it takes special skills and tools to make them edible. Cactus harvesters have to roll the pieces around on the sand and then skin them with a sharp knife to get rid of all the needles and make sure no one gets stabbed.

ESCAPING THE ROCK

School is a little like prison—people tell you what to do, you're confined to campus, and you spend most days wishing you could break free...sort of like these guys.

LIFE ON THE ISLAND

Alcatraz is a 12-acre sandstone island in San Francisco Bay. The city of San Francisco sits just a mile and a half away, but the icy ocean currents near the island are treacherous. In 1934, the U.S. government opened a high-security prison on Alcatraz and started shipping the country's most dangerous criminals there—including famous ones like Al Capone and Machine Gun Kelly.

Officials bragged that Alcatraz was escape-proof, and armed guards watched the inmates' every move. The prisoners—locked in their cells for most of the day— weren't allowed to talk, read newspapers, or listen to the radio. People nicknamed Alcatraz "the Rock," and word leaked out that inmates often went crazy from the boredom and isolation.

Some of the prisoners, though, tried to escape. Most died in the attempt, either shot by guards or drowned in the ocean. But there was one famous escape attempt that may—or may not— have been successful.

The average meteor is about the size of a grain of sand.

A DIABOLICALLY CLEVER PLAN

In 1960, convicted bank robbers Frank Lee Morris and the Anglin brothers—Clarence and John—started plotting a getaway. Each had a small vent in his cell, and the men used nail clippers and spoons stolen from the dining room to pry loose the grills that covered the vents. The goal was to widen the vents and dig a tunnel to the outside. Then they would squeeze through the vents, escape through the tunnel, and use a makeshift raft to sail across the bay to dry land.

Covering up their progress would be hard, but the trio came up with some ingenious ideas:

- They painted pieces of cardboard to look like the grills they'd pried off and then covered their holes with those. Where did they get the cardboard? They made it themselves, by soaking and mashing scraps of paper into a pulp and letting it dry under their mattresses.

- They mixed the excess cement with soap and glue, and then molded the concoction into fake "heads" that they tucked into their beds at night to act as decoys while they were digging. They painted the heads with supplies from an art class and stuck real hair on them that they'd smuggled out of the prison barbershop. The heads fooled the guards for six months while the three men worked.

Each night, they crawled through the vents and crept toward the prison's roof. They worked to pry away the bolts and bend the bars that blocked access to the outside.

Singer Sheryl Crow's two top front teeth are fake.

They also built a raft out of stolen raincoats and stored it in a corridor below the roof.

SO LONG, SUCKERS!

It took two years, but finally, their work was complete. On June 11, 1962, Morris and the Anglins squeezed through the bars, dragged their raft across the roof, and shimmied 50 feet down a drainpipe to the ground. Then they climbed a 15-foot fence topped with barbed wire...and disappeared.

Most people think the trio died in the bay. The water that night was a chilly 50°F, cold enough to cause hypothermia in minutes, and men on a Canadian fishing boat said they saw a body floating facedown in the water soon after. None of the prisoners were heard from again, even though all three had been notorious criminals. FBI investigators didn't think they would just stop committing crimes. So what happened after they got into the water, no one knows. No bodies were ever found. The only trace of them was a black plastic bag with pictures of the Anglin family that washed up near the island a few days later. The fate of the three men remains a mystery.

WRONG FACTS

*Remember: just because you learned
it in school doesn't make it true.*

FACT? *Your hair and fingernails keep growing after you die.*
WRONG! Shortly after death, the human body begins to dry out, especially the skin. This causes it to shrivel and shrink away from the hair and nails, making them look like they're still growing...which they're not.

FACT? *The Wright brothers flew the first aircraft.*
WRONG! In 1904, Wilbur and Orville Wright flew the first aircraft that was capable of being controlled by a human pilot. Gliders and manned kites— which can technically be called "aircraft"—had been flown by dozens of other people over the previous two decades.

FACT? *One dog year is equivalent to seven human years.*
WRONG! This started as a way to compare a dog's life span (about 14 years) with a human lifespan (about 80 years): 14 x 7 = 98. According to researchers today, there is no mathematical correlation between human and dog ages. Based on maturity level, a one-year-old dog is similar to a 15-year-old human; a four-year-old dog is like a 32-year-old human; and a 15-year-old dog is like a 76-year-old human.

A top ping-pong player can hit a ball as fast as 70 mph.

TOY STORIES

*Before PlayStation and cell phones, kids had to make
do with these toys. We bet you'll recognize them.*

RUBIK'S CUBE

If there was one toy that could make a kid in
the 1980s happy, sad, and frustrated all in the
space of a few minutes, it was the Rubik's Cube. Invented by Hungarian sculptor Erno Rubik, the three-inch
cube hooked almost anyone who picked it up. At first,
people just wanted to realign the colored squares, but
then came the competitions, as
solvers raced to outdo each
other. In 2008, Erik Akkers-
dijk from the Netherlands
set a record for solving
the cube: it took him
7.08 seconds. That same
year, 96 people in California set a record for the
most people solving the
cube at once. There's even a
blindfolded competition, in
which contestants get to study
the cube before their eyes are
covered: Ville Sepannen from
Finland holds the current record
for that: 42.01 seconds.

THE HULA HOOP

This toy has been around for centuries—even the ancient Greeks twirled hoops around their waists for fun. But in the late 1950s, the hula hoop was rediscovered by two Americans, Richard Knerr and Arthur "Spud" Melin, who marketed it to kids. Suddenly, hula hooping was a hit, and some people were very good at it: in 1976, eight-year-old Mary Jane Freeze won a hula hoop contest by "hooping" for 10 hours and 47 minutes.

MR. POTATO HEAD

In the 1940s, New York toy inventor George Lerner came up with a brilliant idea: he crafted small eyes, noses, mouths, and ears out of plastic and made dolls for his little sisters by sticking those features onto various vegetables. The potato seemed to work best.

Lerner's sisters loved the potato dolls so much that, in 1949, he tried to sell the concept to several toy companies. They all turned him down—the Great Depression and World War II had ended just a few years before, and many people believed that using vegetables to make toys was wasteful.

Finally, in 1951, Lerner convinced a cereal manufacturer to use the plastic pieces as prizes in its cereal boxes. A year later, the toy company Hasbro decided to sell complete sets of facial features as a toy. It worked: Hasbro sold a million of the toys in the first year, and Mr. Potato Head became a favorite of American children. (The plastic potato body was first included in 1964.)

THE CASE OF THE GOOEY SPITBALL

Here's another classroom mystery. See if you can figure it out. (The answer is on page 243.)

Mr. Patterson was at the blackboard, giving his fifth-grade class a lesson about punctuation. While he was writing on the chalkboard, a gooey spitball hit him in the back of the head.

"Whoa!" said Mr. Patterson, and he turned around to face the class.

He scanned the room and then figured that the culprit had to be sitting in the back row where he (or she) would have the least chance of being seen. Billy, Mark, Melissa, and Danny were sitting back there. And just as Mr. Patterson was about to question the four, Melissa wrote something on a piece of paper, folded it, and raised her hand.

"Yes, Melissa?" said Mr. Patterson.

"May I go to the restroom?" she asked.

"Uh, sure," he said.

On her way out, Melissa slid the folded note onto Mr. Patterson's desk. He quietly picked

George Lucas's inspiration for Chewbacca in *Star Wars*: His dog, Indiana.

it up and turned to face the blackboard again. He unfold-
ed the note and read it. It said: "?! I saw him throw it!"
    Mr. Patterson turned back to the class. "Okay," he
said. "I know who the culprit is."
    How did Mr. Patterson know who threw the spitball?

* * *

AMERICA'S STINGIEST WOMAN

Hetty Green, the heiress to a whaling-business fortune,
was the richest woman in 19th-century America. During
her life, she was worth about $100 million (around $17
billion today), but she spent very little. She lived in tiny
rented rooms, never turned on the heat or used hot
water, ate meat pies that cost about 15 cents each, and
bought new clothes only when her old ones wore out.
    In 1902, Green moved from her home in Vermont
to Hoboken, New Jersey, so she could more closely
manage her money, which was invested in New York's
stock markets. She went to see her stockbrokers every
day and quizzed them about her earnings. Because she
always wore black and lost her temper if she thought
she wasn't making enough money, her bankers gave
her the nickname "the Witch of Wall Street." After
she died in 1916, her two children, Ned and Sylvia,
inherited her fortune, but they didn't inherit her stingi-
ness. Ned loved science and spent most of his money
financing various experiments. Sylvia died in 1951 and
left $800 million to charity.

In 2004, so much gas built up inside a decomposing whale in Taiwan that it exploded.

RUFF POLITICS

Uncle John thinks that animals are our best friends. (Porter the Wonder Dog even has his own ring tone on Uncle John's cell phone.) But this town seems to have gone a little too far.

GOING TO THE DOGS

Sunol is a tiny California suburb, about 40 miles southeast of San Francisco where nothing much ever happens. But in 1981, when faced with two (human) candidates that most residents didn't like, townspeople put Sunol on the map when they elected a Labrador retriever named Bosco as their new mayor.

Bosco's career in politics started one day when two friends were arguing about which one of them could get more votes if they ran for mayor. A third man offered the opinion that his dog, Bosco, could get more votes than either of them. Then, to prove his point, he nominated Bosco for the job.

THE CAMPAIGN TAIL

For several weeks, Bosco campaigned all over town. His stance: He didn't "drink, smoke, or chase women" (he sometimes did chase cars), and he stood for "a bone in every dish, a cat in every tree, and many more fire hydrants." On election day, he won...by a landslide.

Bosco remained the town's mayor for 13 years. It was mostly an honorary title—Sunol had a town council that conducted its business. But the dog did have some "official" duties, including leading the annual Halloween parade. He also rested on a blanket outside a local pub. When a patron had too much to drink, Bosco went for a walk with him until he'd cleared his head.

But the dog's political career wasn't without controversy. In 1989, a newspaper in communist China ran a story attacking the United States and saying that Bosco was an example of how free elections were a failure. The people of Sunol disagreed, of course. They called Bosco "a symbol of democracy and freedom" and said that he represented "individualism and community pride." He even made an appearance at a pro-democracy rally in San Francisco.

LIGHTS OUT

Bosco died in 1994, but Sunol residents didn't want to just let him fade from memory. So they had a bronze statue built in his honor. Today, Mayor Bosco sits forever on his haunches, a kerchief around his neck, keeping watch over the town square.

THIS STORY REALLY STINKS!

Ever run to the bathroom only to find your older sister in there doing her hair—for hours? That's annoying, but imagine if you had to use an outhouse.

WHEN YOU GOTTA GO

Before the days of indoor plumbing, most houses and schools had outhouses—small sheds where people went to the bathroom. An average outhouse was about four feet wide by seven feet tall, and contained a wooden bench with two holes (a large one for adults and a small one for kids) built over a deep pit. Most were simple wooden structures that weren't fixed to the ground. That's because when the outhouse pit filled up, people just covered it with dirt, dug a new pit a few yards away, and moved the structure.

OVER THE MOON

Most outhouses didn't have windows, so people usually carved special holes on the door to let in a little light and air. The shape most associated with an outhouse door is a crescent moon, though no one seems sure why that is. One common explanation says that, in the old days, when most people couldn't read, they needed a way to distinguish the women's outhouse from the

Unlucky in China: The number 4. (The number 8 is lucky.)

men's, if there were two. Men's outhouses usually had a star on them, and women's usually had a crescent moon. And because women tended to take better care of their outhouses, more of those survived.

LOOK OUT BELOW!

Wealthy people sometimes built two-story outhouses for their two-story houses. A bridge led from the house's second floor to the top floor of the outhouse, which had a separate chute down to the pit so people below didn't get an unwelcome...er, shower.

WIPEOUT

Most outhouses didn't come with toilet paper; it was too expensive. Instead, people used old newspapers, catalogs, or magazines to clean up. Some even resorted to corn husks or leaves.

CAN YOU DIG IT?

Here's a great job: "Outhouse diggers" are archaeologists who excavate old outhouse pits. The waste turned into dirt long ago, and the diggers are mostly on the lookout for "treasures" that were tossed down the outhouse hole a hundred years ago or more. What do they find? Usually doll parts, inkwells, marbles, doorknobs, bottles, sword parts, dishes, bone-handled toothbrushes, and false teeth. (Outhouse digger rule: don't bite your fingernails while on the job.)

A WASTEFUL CAREER

In the 1800s, cities hired "nightsoil collectors" to go around to a neighborhood's outhouses at night and collect the waste. You'd think people only did this job long ago, but Brisbane, Australia, had nightsoil collectors on staff until the 1970s.

OUTHOUSE SPEEDWAY

Want to root for outhouses? Take a trip to Trenary, Michigan, which hosts a race called the Outhouse Classic every February. Organizers call it "a real gas," and competitors try to outdo each other by racing their elaborately decorated outhouses down the street. Some of our favorite former entrants: the Flower Power Car Outhouse (decorated to look like a Volkswagen Beetle) and the Vati-Can, which was pushed down the street by a group of nuns.

A piece of unsliced bacon is called a "flitch."

ABRACADABRA! (IT'S SCIENCE)

*How do we know these magic tricks will amaze
and delight your friends? Because
we can read their minds!*

EYE CONTROL YOU

The trick: Tell someone to look straight ahead for a minute and then to look upward with his eyes (without raising his head). Then tell him to close his eyes while still looking up. Now, command him to open his eyelids. Other than some weak eyelid fluttering, your friend won't be able to do it.

How it works: It's simple—if your eyeballs are looking up, your eyelids are physically unable to open.

THAR SHE BLOWS!

The trick: Light a candle (with your parents' help) and set it about eight inches behind a full two-liter bottle of water. Crouch down at table level, and blow really hard against the bottle. Even though the bottle blocks the candle, the flame will still be extinguished.

How it works: It's not magic. The air currents generated by your breath are strong enough to travel around the bottle and put out the candle—it only looks like you blew directly through the bottle.

APPLES AND ORANGES

The trick: Hand your friend an orange and an apple. Tell him to hold one in each hand. Then turn your back. Tell your friend to raise either the apple or the orange into the air and hold that arm straight above his head for about 15 seconds. Then tell him to put his arm down. Now, turn around...and tell him which arm he held up—the apple arm or the orange arm.

How it works: Look for the hand that's lighter in color. Blood will flow out of your friend's hand when it's raised, making it paler than the other hand.

DRY WATER

The trick: This one is pretty cool. First, show your friend a bowl of water. Have him dip his hand in it to see that it is, indeed, a normal bowl of water. Now, dip *your* hand in the water. Remove it...your hand is completely dry!

How it works: Before the trick, rub your hands with talcum powder, which repels water.

STOP TIME

The trick: Find an old wind-up wristwatch and show your audience that it's a working, ticking watch. Then place it on a table and use your magical powers to make it stop ticking.

How it works: Use a table with a tablecloth. Hide a magnet under the tablecloth. When you put the watch on top of the magnet, it will stop the watch. (*Warning:* Be sure your watch is an old, cheap one—when you remove the magnet, it will start ticking again, but sometimes the trick affects the watch's ability to tell accurate time.)

*   *   *

WHAT'S THAT SMELL?

The 16th-century painter Michelangelo had a reputation for being more than an amazing artist—his body odor was so bad, it drove people away. Most Europeans in Michaelangelo's day didn't take baths regularly because they believed that being too clean caused diseases. But the painter seemed smellier than most—while he was working on the Sistine Chapel in Rome, many of his assistants quit because he smelled so bad.

BIG BITES

*These treats might make you wish
you had a bigger mouth.*

FUDGE PHENOM
The world's largest slab of fudge was a swirled vanilla-and-chocolate concoction that weighed more than two tons—as much as a pickup truck! Canada's Northwest Fudge Factory made the mega slab in 2007. It was 166 feet long, 6 feet wide, and 3 inches thick. And it took 86 hours and 13 employees to make it.

LOLLY-PALOOZA

In 2002, Jolly Rancher made the world's largest lollipop, a giant version of its regular-sized cherry lolly. The humongous pop weighed more than 4,000 pounds and was about 19 inches thick. The sucker broke the previous record for the largest lollipop by about 1,000 pounds.

COOKIE MONSTER

Take 30,000 eggs, 12,200 pounds of flour, 6,500 pounds of butter, 6,000 pounds of chocolate chunks, and what do you get? The largest chocolate-chip cookie in the world. The Immaculate Baking Company in Hendersonville, North Carolina, created the cookie, which weighed over 40,000 pounds—more than four large elephants.

MEGA-BURGER

Mallie's Sports Grill and Bar in Southgate, Michigan, boasts the world's largest bacon cheeseburger: 134 pounds, and sitting on a 50-pound bun. According to the restaurant, it takes 12 hours and three men to put the burger together, and it costs $350. (You may want to get a friend to help you eat it.)

CUPCAKE COLOSSUS

Food Network chef Duff Goldman baked a giant cupcake for the show *Ace of Cakes*. The cupcake weighed 61.4 pounds and was more than a foot tall...about 150 times the size of a regular cupcake.

...A rope inside the coffin reached to the surface and was attached to a bell.

BIZARRE NEWS

Even normal people do strange things.

EXCUSE ME...OFFICER?

In January 2009, a 14-year-old boy put on a homemade uniform, walked into a Chicago police station, and successfully impersonated a police officer for five hours before anyone caught on. He was so convincing that he was assigned a partner and sent on patrol. It wasn't until after his "shift" ended that the ruse was discovered: one of the officers noticed that the boy's uniform was missing official patches. It turns out the kid wasn't trying to cause trouble—he was just fascinated by police work. And as for why the police didn't notice he was only 14, one of them said he "looked a lot older."

JUST LET IT GO

A 10-year-old boy named Soski from Glendale, California, got angry while on a walk with his parents. So in a fit of rage, he tossed his teddy bear over a fence—and down a steep canyon. Soski regretted tossing the teddy almost immediately, and his mom agreed to climb down the canyon and get it. Halfway down, she slipped and couldn't climb back up. So his dad went after her—and also slipped. They both ended up trapped 80 feet down, and firefighters had to pull them up with ropes. (And Soski never did get his teddy bear back.)

The words *czar*, *tsar*, *kaiser*, and *July* are all derived from the name Julius Caesar.

ALL ABOARD THE JUNK RAFT!

*These guys took their environmental activism
pretty far...all the way to Hawaii.*

GARBAGE PATCH GUYS

More than 14 billion pounds of trash end up in the world's oceans every year, and a lot of it concentrates in the North Pacific, in an area twice the size of Great Britain called the Great Pacific Garbage Patch.

The Garbage Patch swirls along with the ocean's current, which continuously moves clockwise and catches all kinds of debris (mostly plastic bags, bottles, and wrappers). And once all that trash gets caught in the current, it just stays there, polluting the ocean. So in 2008, two environmentalists named Marcus Eriksen and Joel Paschal built a raft out of trash and sailed it over the Garbage Patch, from California to Hawaii. Why? To try to make people more aware of ocean pollution.

IF YOU BUILD IT...

Eriksen and Paschal's 30-foot "Junk Raft" was made of 15,000 empty plastic bottles. They wrapped the bottles in six large fishing nets to hold them together so the raft would float, used an old airplane cockpit as their cabin, and set up sails to power the raft.

AN INCREDIBLE JOURNEY

On June 1, 2008, the men left Long Beach, California, and planned to take about six weeks to make the 2,600-mile journey. But right away, there were problems. They hadn't glued the tops onto the plastic bottles, and as the raft sailed, the caps started coming off and filling the bottles with water. So the raft started to sink before Eriksen and Paschal even lost sight of the California coastline. Fortunately, Marcus's fianceé lived nearby. She flew in a "rescue mission" via heli-copter and dropped off a glue gun. The guys kept going, but spent the next month gluing the tops onto all the bottles.

Another problem: A few weeks into the trip, they realized they weren't traveling as fast as they'd planned. In fact, they were going only about half as fast. They'd brought enough food for six weeks, but would probably need twice that to complete the trip. So they started eating only half of their food rations each day and caught fish to supplement their diets. But because they were traveling through the Garbage Patch, the fish they caught were often polluted and unappetizing. More than once, they caught a fish, filleted it...and found plastic pieces in its stomach.

MIRACULOUS MEETING

Just when Eriksen and Paschal started to really panic about their food supply, they got some welcome news.

They'd been keeping in touch with the mainland via a computer and satellite phone. The men learned that another small craft was making its way to Hawaii, and it was pretty close to their position.

That craft turned out to belong to Englishwoman Roz Savage ,who was crossing the Pacific Ocean in a rowboat. She wanted to become the first woman to row across the Pacific and, like Eriksen and Paschal, was also trying to highlight the problem of ocean pollution. But she'd run into trouble: Her desalinators had broken and she was nearly out of fresh water. She had food, though. So the two boats met up in the middle of the ocean about 600 miles from Hawaii to swap sea stories, have dinner, and trade supplies. Savage gave the men some food, and they gave her one of their desalinators

ISLAND ARRIVAL

Finally, on August 27, after 88 days at sea, the Junk Raft and its sailors arrived in Honolulu, Hawaii. The first thing Eriksen said when he stepped onto the dock was, "We made it! Where's the food?"

The raft went on display at the Waikiki Aquarium in Honolulu, and the two men planned to make a documentary about the experience. And for their first dinner on dry land? Pizza—quite an improvement over polluted fish, said Eriksen and Paschal.

Fang ("a sweet-smelling fragrance" in Chinese) is a popular name for female cats there.

FART, FART, WHISTLE

Your body can be used to do some incredible things…like make annoying noises in class.

INCREDIBLE JOURNEY
Some kids just seem to have a natural ability to make sounds with their hands, armpits, and mouths. Uncle John was never one of those kids. He tried and tried, but just couldn't do it. So when he became a young man, he traveled to a remote island in the South Pacific and spent 10 years studying under the world's great hand-fart masters. Here's what he learned.

HAND FARTS. Hold out your left hand palm up, with fingers stretched out. Next, place your right hand on top of the left hand crosswise so that the thumb of your right hand touches your left hand where it meets the wrist. Now, squeeze the fingers around the edge of each hand where they touch. Keep your palms cupped together. Next, open the bottom of your hands a little bit to allow air in. Then, squeeze your hands together back into the starting position. The air will get pushed out, making a noise that sounds like a fart. If you don't get it the first time, that's okay. It'll work eventually.

ARMPIT FARTS. Raise up your left arm. Cup your right hand against your left armpit. Lower your left arm quickly, squeezing your right hand against your body. Just like the hand fart, suddenly pushing out the air from a tight space will create a farting noise.

FINGER WHISTLE. Make an "okay" sign with your thumb and index finger. Leave a gap where your two fingers touch—tiny, no more than ⅛ of an inch. Place the fingers barely into your mouth, resting on your bottom lip. Close your lips tightly around the fingers, just enough so that air can flow between the gap in your fingers. Press your tongue against your lower jaw, right behind your bottom teeth. Lightly blow air across the top of your tongue through the finger gap. Adjust your finger, lips, tongue, and how hard you blow to sound a whistle. If you don't get it right away, don't worry—it takes a lot of practice. But take this knowledge with you and let *everybody* hear just how talented (and annoying) you are.

*   *   *

EAT CAKE!

German chocolate cake didn't originate in Germany. It's named after Sam German, an American who invented one of the dessert's original ingredients—the Baker's German's Sweet Chocolate bar—in 1857.

If you lived in Europe before the 1400s, you would never have heard of potatoes or tomatoes.

BEYOND THE WALL

The Berlin Wall was demolished 20 years ago, and few people talk about it today. Why are we talking about it? Because it makes a great escape story.

EAST VS. WEST

Germany's capital is one city today, but in 1948, the country was divided in two: East and West Berlin. That's because the powerful Soviet Union (the United States' ally during World War II, but main enemy after) didn't want to let go of East Berlin, the part of the city it governed when the war ended.

The Soviets were so strict that lots of people living under their rule wanted to leave East Berlin. Many wanted to be reunited with family and friends on the western side. Plus, jobs were hard to come by, food was often scarce, and citizens could be jailed or killed for criticizing the Soviet or East German governments.

TRAPPED!

But no matter how much the East Berliners wanted to leave, the Soviets were determined to stop them. First, the government put up fences and ordered soldiers to shoot anyone who tried to get out. Still, about 2 million people managed to sneak across the border. So in 1961, the Soviets decided to build a concrete wall around the city to keep people in.

The Berlin Wall was under construction for almost 20 years. In the end, it was 10 to 15 feet high, 100 miles long, and topped with barbed wire, mines, guard towers, and electrical booby traps. The Soviets were sure the fortification would keep East Berliners from trying to leave. But between 1961 and 1989, when the wall came down, at least 10,000 people managed to escape to the west...and another 5,000 were arrested or killed trying. Most of the people who outwitted the wall did so during the first two years it was being built. That's because as time went by, the Berlin Wall got longer, wider, and higher.

THE ESCAPE ARTISTS

- An East Berlin butcher once made his own "bullet-proof vest" out of hams and roasts, and then flung himself over the top of the wall. The meat absorbed the bullets and the cuts from the barbed wire. He lived and escaped to the west.

- For years, college students dug tunnels all over East Berlin that reached to the western side. The first tunnel was dug in a graveyard and was disguised to look like a crypt. "Mourners" arrived with flowers and entered the crypt, but they never came out. The East German government finally caught on to this tunnel when a woman went in with her baby but never returned for the stroller she left up top.

- Berlin's sewer system was a popular way to try to escape because the eastern sewers still linked up with the ones in the west. But so many people tried to get out this way that the Soviets eventually cemented all of the city's manhole covers shut and assigned guards to keep watch over the sewers.

- Because the wall went right through the center of the city, there were many buildings that jutted up against it. Parents were known to throw young children out of upper-story windows toward West Berlin, and firemen on the western side would catch them in nets. Other people tossed mattresses over the wall from windows and then jumped to the western side.

- In 1979, eight people flew over the wall in a home-made hot-air balloon. They'd spent months sewing bits of nylon together to make the aircraft. After they succeeded, the East German government kept a close watch on who in the city was buying nylon.

LE McDONALD'S

McDonald's has restaurants all over the world, but in order to succeed, they have to cater to local tastes. The result: some pretty unusual items on the menu.

The Netherlands: The McKrocket, condensed beef gravy that's deep-fried until it's a thick, crispy patty served on a bun.

Germany: Beer and croissants.

India: Most people are Hindu and don't eat beef (cows are sacred in the Hindu religion). A popular menu item is the Maharaja Mac—a Big Mac made with lamb or chicken.

Norway: The McLaks, a grilled salmon sandwich.

Costa Rica: Gallo Pinto, which consists of a cup of seasoned rice and beans.

Greece: Gyros—lamb strips, lettuce, tomato, onions, and a tangy yogurt sauce stuffed into pita bread—is a popular Greek dish. The Greek Mac is made the same way, but with ground beef instead of lamb.

Hong Kong: Instead of being served on buns, the burgers and sandwiches come on sticky rice that's been molded into the shape of a bun.

Singapore: Popular items include the Kampung Burger, a sausage patty topped with sliced chicken and pineapple served on an English muffin; and the McTowkay

Burger, a patty of eggs and marinated ground beef mixed together and served on a bun.

Thailand: The Samurai Pork Burger (it's teriyaki-flavored). And for dessert, Sweet Corn Pie.

Spain: Gazpacho, which is a raw vegetable (mostly tomato) soup, always served ice-cold.

Canada: Poutine, french fries covered in cheese and gravy.

Philippines: McSpaghetti—spaghetti, tomato sauce, and hot-dog chunks.

Italy: The Fiodiriso Salad, made of lettuce, rice, tuna, mushrooms, and ham.

Uruguay: The McHuevo, a hamburger topped with a poached egg.

Japan: You can order the Ebi Filet-O (a shrimp burger), the Koroke Burger (a sandwich of mashed potato, cabbage, and sauce), the Ebi-Chiki (deep-fried shrimp nuggets), or a macaroni-and-cheese sandwich...and wash it down with a green tea–flavored milk shake.

* * *

POP QUIZ

A mother of four hungry children has only three potatoes. Without using fractions, can you figure out how she can feed all of them and still serve each child an equal amount of potatoes? (*The answer is on page 242.*)

FIRST DAY ON THE JOB

Want to grow up to be president? It's a big job...with a big first day.

T**HE MOMENT ARRIVES**
Today, presidential inaugurations take place on January 20, but it wasn't always that way. George Washington's first inaugural was on April 30, 1789, and subsequent inaugurations took place in March. It wasn't until the 20th Amendment to the U.S. Constitution was ratified in 1933 that January 20 was chosen as inauguration day. The amendment says that a president's term "shall end at noon on the 20th day of January." Congress decided on the date change because it felt that swearing in presidents in March or April, when they were elected in November, made voters wait too long for their new leader. In 1937, Franklin Delano Roosevelt was the first president to be inaugurated on the new date.

THE LONG AND SHORT OF IT

George Washington gets the award for the shortest inaugural speech. His second address, delivered on March 4, 1793, was just 135 words long.

On the other hand, William Henry Harrison gave

the longest in 1841—it ran more than 8,000 words and lasted for two hours. According to many, the speech also contributed to Harrison's death. Speaking outdoors on that cold March day, Harrison refused to wear a hat, coat, or gloves. A result: he caught pneumonia and died a month later, making his the shortest presidency.

FIRST THINGS FIRST

Presidential inaugurations have been going on for more than 200 years, so it makes sense that they've incorporated new technology. Here are a few inauguration firsts:

- The first floats in the inaugural parade (Martin Van Buren, 1837)

- The first photograph of the event (James Buchanan, 1857)

- The first motion picture (William McKinley, 1897)

- The first use of an automobile to bring the president to the event (Warren G. Harding, 1921)

- The first radio broadcast (Calvin Coolidge, 1925)

- The first talking film of the event (Herbert Hoover, 1929)

- The first televised inauguration (Harry S. Truman, 1949)

- The first color broadcast (John F. Kennedy, 1961)

- And the first Internet broadcast (Bill Clinton, 1997)

AN UNWELCOME GUEST

John Wilkes Booth attended Abraham Lincoln's second inauguration. At least one person remembered seeing him there, and Booth and several of his conspirators appear in photographs taken on that day in 1865—less than two months before he assassinated Lincoln.

A NEW LEGACY

The first president sworn in while wearing long pants: John Quincy Adams on March 4, 1825. The presidents before him wore knickers and stockings, which were common in the 18th and early 19th centuries.

*　*　*

DID YOU KNOW?

- The Baby Ruth candy bar was named for President Grover Cleveland's daughter Ruth.

- President Zachary Taylor never actually voted in a presidential election.

Komodo dragons have been known to prey on deer, horses, and water buffalo.

RECORD BREAKERS

Some kids might be even weirder than you are.

- **Praveen Kumar Sehrawat**, 16, can spray a stream of milk a record 12 feet. But he doesn't do it through his mouth or even his nose. He sucks milk up through his nostrils and then shoots it out of the tear ducts in his eyes! Sehrawat, who lives in India, also holds his country's record for eating green chilies: 170 in five minutes.

- **Students at King Edward's School** in Edgbaston, England, collected more than 28,000 socks and 24,500 clothespins. Then they hung all the socks on a line and set the record for the world's longest clothesline of socks: 0.8 mile.

- New Zealand teenager **Elliot Nicholls** set a record for sending text messages while blindfolded. The previous record was a 160-letter message sent in 83 seconds. Nicholls did it in just 45 seconds.

- Eight-year-old **Aman Rehman** of Dehra Dun, India, is the world's youngest college lecturer. He is a computer genius who teaches digital animation classes at a local art school.

- **Tiana Walton**, 9, from Cheshire, England, broke the record for "most snails sitting on a human face." A grand total of 25 slimed around Walton's face for 10 seconds, outpacing the previous record of 15 snails.

Longest-running prime-time animated TV series: *The Simpsons*, which debuted in 1989.

BLOOPER REEL

Film directors work hard on their movies,
but they still make mistakes.

- In **Star Wars: A New Hope**, the storm troopers break into the Death Star's control room looking for C-3PO, and one of the troopers hits his head on the door frame.

- Look carefully at the scene in **Harry Potter and the Chamber of Secrets** when Harry fights the basilisk. There's a safety tip on the end of his sword.

- In **High School Musical 2**, just before the kids start singing "What Time Is It?" Troy's boxers show above his waistband—but they change from white to a dark color a moment later.

- When Batman interrogates the Joker in **The Dark Knight**, the camera crew's reflection appears briefly in the two-way mirror.

- At the beginning of **I Am Legend**, all the bridges into Manhattan are destroyed, but at the end, two characters leave the city by driving over a bridge.

FLYING HIGH

How much of your school day is spent staring out the window, watching the flag wave in the wind? Here's some history about what you're looking at.

OLD GLORY

- You may have heard that Betsy Ross designed the American flag—she didn't. Her grandson spread that rumor in the 1870s. No one knows for sure who came up with the design, but many historians now believe it was a 1770s congressman from New Jersey named Francis Hopkinson.

- Only the president or a state governor may order that the American flag be flown at half-mast. It's usually done as a way to honor a former president, vice president, Supreme Court justice, member of Congress, or military leader who has died. But sometimes other figures and events are honored this way, too: President George W. Bush ordered that the flag be flown at half-mast in 2002 on the first anniversary of the 9/11 attacks and again in 2005, when civil rights activist Rosa Parks died.

- The flag flies over the White House only if the president is in Washington, D.C. If he's away, no flag.

STATE FLAGS

- Oregon is the only state whose flag has a different

design on the back. The front shows the state seal with the words "State of Oregon," and the year "1859," when it became part of the United States. On the back is a beaver, the state animal.

- Ohio is the only state whose flag isn't rectangular—it's a pennant shape.

- In 1927, the Alaska Territory held a contest to design its flag (though it didn't become a state until 1959). The winner was 13-year-old John Benson. The design: a blue background with one large star in the upper right corner and seven smaller stars forming the Big Dipper in the middle. It's still the state's flag today.

- Canada didn't get an official national flag until 1965.

- Washington's state flag is the only one with a portrait of a person on it. (That person is, naturally, George Washington.)

- Only one country in the world has a flag that's a solid block of color—the flag of the African nation of Libya is all green.

- In 1846, artist William Todd took on the task of designing a flag for California. He was supposed to draw a pear in the middle of a banner. (Northern California has lots of pear orchards.) But due to smeared ink on the written request (or bad handwriting), Todd thought it said "bear." So that's what he drew, and it's still on the flag today.

X-TREME EATING

If becoming a pro athlete seems beyond your reach, don't despair. You might be able to train your stomach for victory instead.

BURGERS AND DOGS
In 2006, Takeru "Tsunami" Kobayashi of Japan won $10,000 for eating 97 hamburgers in eight minutes. He's also put away 58 bratwursts in 10 minutes to win the Nathan's Famous Hot Dog Eating Contest in Coney Island, New York. (He's won the contest seven times in the last eight years.)

PIZZA AND WINGS
The only man to defeat "Tsunami" at Coney Island: Joey Chestnut, who is also a world-champion pizza eater and holds the record for speed-eating chicken wings, 182 in 30 minutes.

CHILI AND PEPPERS
Rich "Locust" LeFevre, who is in his 60s, holds the world records for devouring chili (1½ gallons in 10 minutes) and pickled jalapeño peppers (247 in 8 minutes).

LOBSTERS AND MORE
In 2005, Sonya "Black Widow" Thomas gobbled up 44

lobsters in 12 minutes to win Maine's World Lobster-Eating Championship. She also holds the world record for fruitcake, meatballs, cheesecake, eggs, and chili cheese fries. Oh—and she weighs just 105 pounds.

OYSTERS AND PICKLED JALAPEÑOS

In April 2008, when Patrick "Deep Dish" Bertoletti was just 23 years old, he became the world's oyster-eating champion after downing 34 dozen raw oysters in eight minutes. He also challenged "Locust" LeFevre's pickled jalapeño record in 2008 (he ate 191 in 6½ minutes), but didn't beat it. He graduated from college with a degree in—what else—culinary arts!

...Its events include pig-racing, pig-swimming, and pigball.

SADDLE UP!

*In movies, cowboys are usually portrayed by white
men, but in reality, about 25 percent of them were
African American. Here's the Wild West story
of history's most famous black cowboy.*

LEARNING THE ROPES

Bill Pickett was born in Texas in 1870, the son of
two former slaves. There were 13 children in the
Pickett family, and there wasn't much time for school.
So Bill dropped out when he was 10 and got his first
job—as a ranch hand.

The work was hard: Bill cleaned up around the place,
fed the animals, and mucked out the stalls. But it
brought him close to the horses, and he soon taught
himself how to rope and ride.

PAYING HIS DUES

It wasn't long before Pickett started putting on amateur
shows around town, performing rodeo tricks for people
on the street and passing around a hat to collect
donations. For the next 20 years, he moved all over
Texas, working as a cowboy—rounding up cattle and
breaking horses—and putting on shows to make extra
money. He and his brothers even started their own
horse-breaking and ranching company: the Pickett
Brothers Bronco Busters and Rough Riders Association.

STEER WRASSLIN'

During these years, Pickett perfected his rodeo techniques. His most impressive skill: a new trick called
"bulldogging." Today it's known as steer wrestling, and
here's how it works: A cowboy on horseback races along
next to a running steer. At just the right moment, he
slides off of his horse, tackles the steer, and wrestles it
to the ground.

There are lots of stories about how Bill Pickett came
up with the bulldogging technique, but the most common one says that in 1903, while he was working at a
ranch in Rockdale, Texas, Pickett came across a steer
that just wouldn't cooperate with him. The animal was
running around the ranch, refusing to go into the corral, and antagonizing the entire herd of cattle. Pickett
finally got fed up with the beast, raced him on horseback at full speed, and then tackled him. Still, the
animal wouldn't calm down, so Pickett
bit him hard on the lower lip and took
him to the ground.

RODEO ROYALTY

Today, steer wrestling is a
common rodeo event
(even though rodeo riders
don't bite steers on the lip).
But when Bill Pickett introduced the technique in the
early 1900s, no one had seen

Old fogy: The computer mouse was introduced in 1968.

it before, and people were fascinated. He became so famous that, in 1905, he moved to Oklahoma and signed up with one of America's most prestigious Wild West shows: the Miller Brothers 101 Ranch Show.

One of his colleagues in the show was "Buffalo" Bill Cody.

But still, many rodeo competitions wouldn't let Pickett enter because he was black. So the management at the 101 Ranch often billed him as an American Indian. (He did have some Cherokee ancestry.)

LAST RIDE

Pickett worked for the 101 Ranch for almost 30 years. He performed in Mexico, Canada, South America, England, and the United States. But in 1932, he died after an accident in which one of the horses at the ranch kicked him hard in the head.

More than 50 years later, though, his legacy as the most famous black cowboy lives on: the Bill Pickett Invitational Rodeo, formed in 1984, is the only all-African American touring rodeo in the United States.

*   *   *

Cowboy proverb: Never kick a cow chip on a hot day.

DIG LIKE AN EGYPTIAN

What does Egypt make you think of? Pyramids, of course. There are lots of them...and people keep finding more.

OFFICIAL TREASURE HUNTERS
Egypt has such a strong connection to its ancient culture that the country employs a high-ranking government official to discover and preserve artifacts. That person is Zahi Hawass, chief of antiquities. His job: to take teams of archaeologists into the Egyptian desert to uncover ancient tombs and pyramids.

In 2006, Hawass and his team of diggers started excavating in Saqqara, an area about 18 miles south of Cairo. Today, it's a scientific site, but in ancient Egypt, Saqqara was a huge burial ground for pharaohs and other VIPs from the Egyptian capital city of Memphis.

DIG ON!

Hawass and his crew dug for two years with little success. They weren't surprised; Saqqara had been an archaeological site for decades, and most scientists thought it had already been completely excavated. But finally, in November 2008, Hawass's team found something. Sixty-five feet below the sand, they uncovered a 16-foot-tall section of a pyramid that was more than 4,000 years old and had once stood 45 feet high. The markings on the pyramid's walls indicated that it was the resting place of Queen Sesheshet, the mother of Teti, founder of Egypt's sixth dynasty.

Grave robbers had stripped the pyramid of its jewels and other treasure long ago, probably just a few hundred years after it was built. But the scientists kept digging... and looking.

Finally, in January 2009, they came across something incredible: Sesheshet's mummy. Not the whole mummy, but parts of it—a skull and many bones. Both the pyramid and the mummy were great finds because very few of ancient Egypt's pyramids were dedicated to women. They were mostly reserved for male royalty. According to Hawass, "You can discover a tomb or a statue, but to discover a pyramid, it makes you happy. And a pyramid of a queen—queens have magic."

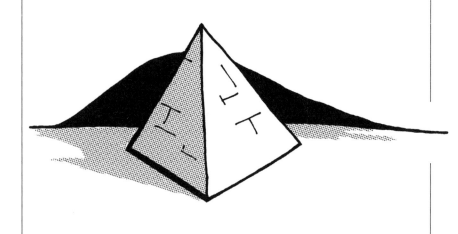

The center on a football team was once called the "snapper-back."

HOLE IN ONE

Psst! Nobody loves doughnuts more than Uncle John. Whenever anyone brings a box of them to the BRI, it mysteriously disappears.

HISTORIC EATS

Doughnuts have been around for centuries—scientists have even found fossilized fried dough in ancient American Indian ruins. The word first appeared in writing in 1803, when an English cookbook included a recipe for doughnuts. And in America, author Washington Irving published *A Knickerbocker's History of New York* in 1809. The book told funny stories about the city's Dutch settlers. In it, he wrote about "balls of sweetened dough, fried in hog's fat, and called doughnuts."

DOUGH-NUT OR DOUGH-KNOT?

Those early doughnuts were called *olykoeks* ("oily cakes" in Dutch), and they didn't have holes in the middle. They usually had a nut at the center because the dough in the middle of the balls didn't cook thoroughly, and the nuts made the gooey centers tastier.

Some people believe that's why the olykoek eventually got a name change: a dough-nut. But others think the name came from the fact that the pastries were sometimes braided or twisted into dough-knots.

THE CAPTAIN'S SWEET MISSION

In 1847, an American sea captain named Hanson Gregory invented the doughnut hole. His mother, Elizabeth, was well-known throughout New England for her olykoeks. (Legend has it that hers were especially delicious because she added nutmeg to the dough and used hazelnuts for the center.) But Captain Gregory didn't like the pastries' soggy middles. On one sea voyage, he started cutting them out with the round top of a pepper tin and throwing them away.

When he got home and showed his mother the technique, she started cutting out the centers before frying the dough. And she discovered that if she did that, the pastry cooked all the way through.

DOUGHNUTS GO TO WAR

Over the next few decades, doughnuts with holes caught on all over the United States. During World War I, a group of women from the Salvation Army were in France, trying to help make the soldiers feel at home. In the summer of 1917, a unit near Montiers was soaked from 36 days of rain, and the women decided to make doughnuts to cheer everybody up. They rolled the dough with an old wine bottle, cut the doughnuts with the top of a baking soda tin, and deep-fried the dough in a soldier's helmet, seven at a time. The men loved them.

That first day, the women made only 100 doughnuts, but they were soon making and serving doughnuts 24 hours a day, frying them up in several helmets. And they made huge batches—their standard recipe called for eight eggs and 18 cups of flour, and the doughnuts were fried in five pounds of lard.

HOMECOMING

After the war, the troops came home and wanted more doughnuts. So a man named Adolph Levitt answered their doughnut obsession—he invented a machine for mass-producing them in 1920. It went on display at the 1934 World's Fair in Chicago, where the doughnut was hailed there as a "hit food." Next came the doughnut shops: Krispy Kreme started selling them in 1937, and Dunkin' Donuts opened in 1950.

Today, more than 10 billion are sold every year in the United States and Canada. But as people pay more attention to their diets, many have begun worrying that doughnuts are unhealthy. Those with a sweet tooth need not fear too much. An average doughnut has about 300 calories; an average bagel with cream cheese has 450. So as long as you don't overdo it, go ahead!

KIDS RULE!

Some people say that you won't get anywhere in this world without years of hard work. But these kids prove that when you really love something, success can come early.

STOKED!

John John Florence rode on his first surfboard when he was six months old. Okay...his dad was with him, but by the time he was five, he was surfing alone at Hawaii's Bonzai Pipeline, one of the most dangerous surfing spots in the world. In the winter, waves there can swell up to 30 feet high. In 2005, when he was just 13 years old, John John qualified for the Triple Crown of Surfing, a three-part competition that many people consider the sport's most prestigious professional event. John John was the youngest person ever to compete in the contest, and even though he didn't get past the first round, he did score higher than some pros twice his age.

Surfing isn't John John's only hobby, though. He's also a skilled skateboarder and snowboarder who has competed for the title of "Ultimate Boarder," a surfing/skateboarding/snowboarding competition in Santa Barbara, California.

GUITAR HERO

Tallan Latz (known as T-Man) likes to ride his bike and play sports like other kids, but he'd rather be inside his

Wisconsin home, wearing cool black shades and practicing his electric guitar. At nine years old, T-Man is the youngest professional blues guitarist in the world today, and his riffs are so good that he's jammed with rock legend Jackson Browne and played at Chicago's famous House of Blues. All that didn't come easy, though. He's been playing the electric guitar since he was four and practices for two to three hours every day. But T-Man says it's all worth it: "I just love to play the guitar. It's my favorite feeling."

A REAL MASTERPIECE

When Akiane Kramarik turned 14 in 2008, she'd already been a professional painter for seven years. She made her first drawing—of an angel—when she was four and gave it to her mom as a present. When she was seven, she painted a self-portrait and sold it for $10,000!

Akiane is homeschooled in Idaho so she can spend most of her days painting. But as much as she loves art, there's even more she wants to accomplish. She especially wants to help people living in poverty in Lithuania, where her parents grew up. She says, "They need help with food and medicine, and a free hospital. I really want to build a free hospital for them." Good luck, Akiane!

*   *   *

Misnamed: Greenland is mostly snow and ice. Iceland is mostly green.

TOYS = MONEY IN THE BANK

Don't let your mom throw away your stuff—you never know what might become a "collectible."

ACTION FIGURE
In 2002, an original 1963 G.I. Joe was sold to the Geppi Museum in Baltimore, Maryland. Price: $200,000.

YO-YO

In 1974, President Richard Nixon autographed a yo-yo for country music star Roy Acuff. After Acuff died in 1992, the yo-yo sold at an auction for $16,000.

BARBIE DOLL

In 2003, an original 1959 Barbie doll (still in the box) sold for $25,427.

BASEBALL CARD

The rarest card—only six perfect copies exist—is known as the 1909 Honus Wagner "T206." Why is it so rare? Wagner, a Hall of Famer who played mostly for the Pittsburgh Pirates, was strongly opposed to cigarette smoking, and he had the card canceled because it was

---

Panda car: British slang for a police car (because it's black and white).

manufactured by a tobacco company. In 2007, one of the cards sold at an auction for $2.8 million.

COMIC BOOK

The most ever paid for a comic book was for a 1938 *Action Comics #1*. The issue contained the first-ever appearance of Superman. Price: $317,200. (The owner, who'd had the comic since he was nine, bought it for 35 cents in the 1950s.)

PEZ DISPENSER

PEZ manufactured two dispensers shaped like astronauts to be sold at the 1982 World's Fair. They later scrapped the idea. In 2006, one of the two prototypes sold on eBay for $32,000.

CANDY

A single brown M&M that had been on a 2004 space-flight sold for $1,500.

* * *

SLICE IT THICK

In 1946, the *New York Times* heralded a "new style in peanut butter," telling readers that "instead of scooping peanut butter out of a jar to spread on crackers and bread, [they] might soon be slicing it from a brick, much as we now do cheese." Alas, the innovation, from scientists at Georgia State College, never caught on.

DIRTY WORK

These jobs are dirty, but somebody's got to do them.
And hey—who knows, maybe you'll find your calling.

DOG BREATH SNIFFERS

Some people make a living by putting their noses in front of a dog's mouth and smelling. Then they grade the smelliness of the dog's breath on a scale of 0 to 10 and put it into categories like sweaty, salty, musty, fungal, or decaying. After the first round of sniffing, the dog gets a fresh-breath treat or some food, and the sniffer tries again. The dog sniffer's job is to test how well the treats or different types of dog food change (and hopefully improve) the smell of the dog's breath.

Unlike most cats, the spotted ocelot loves to swim.

PEOPLE SNIFFER

If you have a good nose but don't like the idea of smelling dog breath, you can always use your sniffing skills to smell human breath instead. Breath odor evaluators smell nasty morning breath, garlic breath, coffee breath, and other stenches and rate them on a scale from 1 to 9 (with 1 being the stinkiest). Then the evaluator smells and rates the breath again after the person has used products like mints, gum, or mouthwash, which is how the manufacturers test the effectiveness of their products.

DEAD BODY PREPARERS

A *diener*, from the German word for "servant," prepares corpses for autopsies and for doctors who study the effects of deadly diseases on human bodies. Dieners cut up dead bodies and remove their organs so that the doctors can weigh and examine them. People in this line of work wear scrubs, an apron, gloves, surgical boots, hairnets, goggles, and masks to protect them from the blood, guts, and smells of the dead bodies.

PORTABLE TOILET CLEANERS

Portable toilets aren't much fun to use, but imagine if you had to clean them for a living. Most workers clean 10 to 60 of them a day. Of course, how many they can clean in a day depends on how dirty the toilet is. How do they do it? They pick up stray toilet paper and wash down the floor and walls using a high-pressure hose.

Then they use a tank and vacuum wand to suck up all the waste. It's a dirty job, but the pay isn't bad: portable toilet cleaners can make up to $50,000 a year.

POOPER SCOOPERS

Want an outside job on an exotic island in the fresh air? Get a job collecting guano (or, bird poop) off the coast of Peru. Why would anyone do that? Companies use the guano to make fertilizer. Dung collectors wake up at 3:30, grab a shovel and pickax, and spend the next 12 hours hacking away at hardened seabird poop on rock-hard soil.

After scraping up the dung, they collect it, sift and filter it through a piece of wire mesh, bag it, and pile the bags onto barges. The barges then carry the precious cargo to the mainland.

It's a dirty job. Most workers go barefoot, so their feet and legs are coated with a layer of poop by the end of the day. And some wear handkerchiefs to avoid breathing in dung dust.

In a year, a work crew usually collects about 15,000 tons of precious bird poop, which brings in a lot of money. A ton of Peruvian guano can sell for up to $500.

* * *

WORLD'S SMALLEST WINGED INSECT

The Tanzanian parasitic wasp is just 0.2 millimeter... about the same size as a housefly's eye.

HOBO SLANG

In the early 20th century, homeless people—known then as hobos—traveled around the country by stowing away in trains. They also had their own colorful lingo.

Wood butcher: a carpenter

Black strap: coffee

Hundred on a plate: a can of beans

Saddle blankets: pancakes

Tin roof: a free meal

Wind pudding: air; having nothing to eat is "living on wind pudding"

Baldy: an old man

Comet: a new hobo

Fingy: a hobo who is missing fingers

Paul Bunyan: an entertaining liar

Yegg: a criminal

Coop: a jail

Bone orchard: a graveyard

Cozzy: a public restroom

Crowbar hotel: a police station

Doghouse: a caboose

Flop: sleep

Gooseberry: to steal clothes off a clothesline

Padding the hoof: traveling by foot

Bindle: a pack carried over the shoulder

California blanket: a newspaper

Grinders: teeth

Polish the mug: wash your face

Throw the guts: to talk too much

HOW TO MAKE A BLOODY EYEBALL

Halloween is supposed to be fun, and we bet it would be super fun to see real bloody eyeballs at your school's next Halloween party. The teachers might object, though, so here's a recipe for bloody eyeball ice cubes that's sure to make them say "Ewww!"

WHAT YOU'LL NEED

- 15–20 radishes
- 15–20 green olives, stuffed with pimientos
- Water
- An empty ice tray
- A vegetable peeler

GETTING STARTED:

- You'll want to prepare your eyeballs at least one day before you need them, and be sure to get your parents' permission before you do any cutting.

An adult human eyeball is about two-thirds the size of a ping-pong ball.

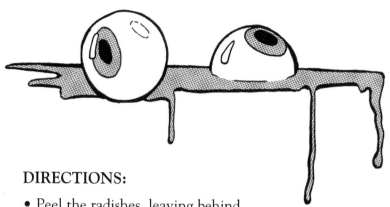

DIRECTIONS:

- Peel the radishes, leaving behind thin streaks of the red skin to look like blood vessels.

- Using the end of the vegetable peeler, cut a small hole in each radish—about the size of an olive.

- Stuff one olive (pimiento side out) into each radish.

- Put one radish in each section of the empty ice tray.

- Fill the tray with water, freeze overnight, and voilà! Your bloody eyeballs are ready for school.

* * *

THREE THINGS PRESIDENTS CAN'T DO?

- Swim naked. Wrong!—John Quincy Adams liked to go skinny-dipping in the Potomac River.

- Dress casually. Wrong!—Thomas Jefferson often wore pajamas when greeting visitors.

- Overeat. Wrong!—William Howard Taft was so fat (about 325 pounds) that he got stuck in the bathtub at the White House...more than once.

The *Mona Lisa* isn't painted on canvas—it's painted on a wood panel.

ANIMAL CRAZY

We bet even your teacher won't be able to get all of these animal questions right. Quiz her and see.

Q. What amphibian's face looks like Humpty Dumpty?
A. The Mexican axolotl, a type of salamander, has a face that many scientists describe as looking like an unbroken egg. It's called a "walking fish" because it lives mostly in water, but has four legs. Adding to its odd appearance—a long fin and feathery gills that stick out of its head like antenna. These creatures generally grow to be about one foot long and can live for up to 15 years. Wild Mexican axolotls are found only near Lake Xochimilco, not far from Mexico City.

Q. What shell-covered mammal can virtually disappear before your eyes?
A. When feeling threatened, the pink fairy armadillo can dig itself into a hole in just a few seconds. This exotic little creature lives only in central Argentina. It's the smallest member of the armadillo family (about four inches long) and has a pinkish armor shell. Underneath the shell, the animal is covered with white hairs. Pink fairy armadillos prefer dry, warm places and usually burrow near anthills because they like to munch on ants and ant larvae.

Q. *What tiny creature oozes stinky goop from its skin?*
A. The warty newt. This small lizardlike European animal has glands in its skin that secrete a foul-smelling, milky goo to keep its enemies away. Most warty newts grow to be about seven inches long. They're nocturnal—which means they're awake and hunting at night—and they spend about six months of the year hibernating. Another amazing ability: they can regrow missing body parts.

Q. *What living thing has no heart, no blood, no brain, and no bones?*
A. A jellyfish...and the Arctic lion's mane jellyfish is the world's largest. Its blobby body can be eight feet long, with tentacles that float behind it another 100 feet or so. These jellyfish live in the cold waters of the North Atlantic and Arctic oceans. They aren't strong swimmers, so they usually float close to the surface and let the ocean's currents carry them along. Like all jelly-fish, the Arctic lion's mane jellyfish is made up of 95 per-cent water. The species

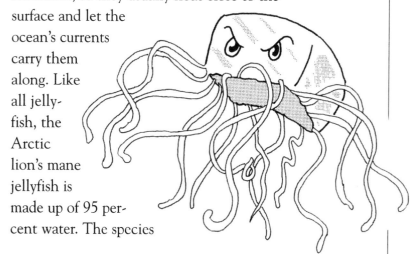

has been around for about 650 million years—since long before the dinosaurs.

Q. What large amphibian can't get any shut-eye?
A. It's tough for Chinese giant salamanders to close their eyes—they have no eyelids. These big guys hail from China (of course) and live in fast-moving streams and rivers. They usually grow to be more than three feet long—some stretch as long as six feet—making them the largest salamanders in the world.

Q. What animal rotates its feet?
A. The kinkajou—a little mammal that grows to be about 20 inches long and lives in rain forests from southern Mexico to Brazil—can rotate its feet and turn around by simply pointing them forward or backward. These fruit-eating animals, which are related to rac-coons, have long tails, similar to those of monkeys, that help them balance and hang from trees. And their tongues, which measure about five inches long, help them suck up flower nectar and honey to keep up their energy level (and satisfy their sweet tooth).

* * *

"Part of being a winner is knowing when enough is enough. Sometimes you have to give up the fight and walk away, and move on to something that's more productive." **—Donald Trump**

The word *hiccup* has been in use since 1530.

FART FACTS

If you're average, you fart between 14 and 23 times a day. If you fart more than that, here are two things you might want to know.

- Farts are the result of air or gas getting into your intestines. How does it get in there? Sometimes—like when you're eating—you swallow air. People who chew gum, eat with their mouths open, smoke, or suck on candy fart more than people who don't because they swallow more air.

- Also, your stomach produces gas when it digests food. That's why there are two types of farts: stinky ones and odorless ones. The stinky ones smell bad because of sulfur gas that's released after you eat certain foods. Cheese and meat have a lot of sulfur in them, so those farts are more likely to smell. Beans can make you really gassy, but most of them don't have much sulfur. So bean farts don't usually smell too bad. (Of course, if you add a lot of cheese to your beans, it's another story.)

Actress Natalie Portman was born in Jerusalem.

CHEATERS WHO WON

Here are the true stories of two notorious crooks who turned their bad habits into (honest) fame and fortune.

CATCH HIM IF YOU CAN

One of history's most notorious cheaters is probably Frank Abagnale Jr. In the 1960s, he went on a worldwide crime spree of frauds, cons, and forgeries that stumped the FBI for years and earned Frank more than $2 million.

The first person he conned: his dad. When he was a teenager in the early 1960s, Abagnale convinced gas station owners to charge fake purchases to his dad's credit card and then give Abagnale the money instead. The charges showed up as tires or gas, and Abagnale used the cash to buy presents for his girlfriends. From there, he went on to cash forged checks at banks around the world and to perfect his impersonations. Between 1964 and 1969, he passed himself off as a university professor, a lawyer, a pediatrician, and a pilot for Pan Am Airways. He always changed his name and stayed a few steps ahead of the FBI.

But in 1969, when Abagnale was 21 years old, a man in France recognized him from a wanted poster. The French police finally caught him and eventually sent him back to the United States for a trial. He spent less than five years in prison, though, because he agreed to help the FBI track other forgers and crooks. One of the conditions of that job? He couldn't get paid. So he started his own business (to help companies protect themselves from fraud) and wrote a book about his crimes, called *Catch Me If You Can*. That book became a movie in 2002, starring Leonardo DiCaprio.

And just for the record, Frank Abagnale Jr. didn't always cheat. He legitimately passed the Louisiana bar exam when he was 19...or so he says.

THIS GUY CAN HACK IT

Kevin Mitnick started hacking into computers when he was 12. That's when he figured out how to rig his bus pass to get free rides on the Los Angeles transit system. Then in high school, he used a computer to make free long-distance telephone calls. By the time he was in his 20s, he was using the Internet to steal cell-phone service and breaking into companies' computer systems to steal their software.

He was arrested twice, in 1988 and 1995. The second time, he went to jail for five years and was on probation for another eight. The rules of his probation: he couldn't use the Internet at all for the entire time.

Today, all that's behind him, and Mitnick runs a computer security company in Nevada. His clients actually *pay* him to break into their computers—but now it's to find out how real hackers might do it so the companies can protect themselves against computer crime.

ONLINE FUN

When Uncle John gets tired of writing and feels like goofing off, where does he go? To some of his favorite Web sites.

PANDORA

Tell Pandora what bands you like, and it tailors a streaming audio feed for you based on those. It's like your very own radio station where you hear the music you like and discover new, similar music you'll probably like too. (pandora.com)

EHOW

You can learn how to do virtually anything here—from how to take a photograph to how to potty-train your new puppy. (*ehow.com*)

KONGREGATE

Hundreds of video games you can play for free online. 'Nuff said. (*kongregate.com*)

You can buy emu jerky from Australian vending machines.

I LIKE TOTALLY LOVE IT!

This is a site full of ridiculous stuff you didn't know existed that might become ridiculous stuff you absolutely must have. For example: a bar of soap that looks like a Popsicle, a wallet that looks like a piece of toast, and hot pink toilet paper. (*iliketotallyloveit.com*)

VIRTUAL BUBBLEWRAP

Do you think the best part about getting a package is popping the bubble wrap? (We do.) Well, on this site, you can pop all the bubbles you want. All you have to do is point your mouse at the bubble you want to pop and click—it pops! The bubble even makes that great popping sound and looks "popped" when you're done. It also includes a timer to try to beat your time for completing a whole "sheet." Pop till you drop! (*virtual-bubblewrap.com*)

SPORCLE

This site is home to hundreds of quizzes on every subject, from history and geography to music and sports. Can you name all the presidents, planets, and *Sesame Street* characters in the time provided? (*sporcle.com*)

FUNOLOGY

Bored? This Web site has plenty of ideas for things to do to pass the time...and almost all of them involve *not* sitting at a computer. You'll find things like puzzles, magic tricks, science experiments, and scavenger hunts. (*funology.com*)

WILD (WEST) CHILD

You may know that Buffalo Bill Cody became famous for his rodeo tricks. But few people know he went on a heroic journey when he was just 10 years old.

ROUGH BEGINNINGS

Bill Cody grew up in Kansas in the 1850s. Back then, the area was a battleground for the fight over slavery. The violence became so intense that people called the state "Bleeding Kansas."

Bill's father, Isaac Cody, opposed slavery. But the family's neighbors were mostly for it, and often used violence to intimidate people who disagreed with them. When Bill was eight, several neighbors stabbed his father during a town meeting. Isaac Cody didn't die, but he received even more death threats, and that drove him into hiding.

The rest of the family stayed on their farm, and over the next few months, pro-slavery raiders stole their horses and livestock. Other gangs set their crops on fire.

BOY HERO

Two years passed, but the bad blood between the two groups continued. One day, when 10-year-old Bill was at home and sick with the flu, he overheard a friend tell his mother that pro-slavery hoodlums had tracked down his father and planned to ambush him. So the boy got up, saddled his horse, and took off to warn his father. After Bill had ridden for eight miles, the gang started chasing him. But the boy kept going.

Bill dug in his spurs and made it nine more miles to a friend's house. His pursuers finally ran off, but by then, Bill was very sick—he'd thrown up and could barely stand. So he spent the night with his friend and took off again in the morning. He reached his father the next day—and the gang started chasing him again. But he and his dad hid out until the men were gone.

THE REST OF THE STORY

Bill Cody grew up to live a wild life. He was a scout for the U.S. Army and a buffalo hunter—that's how he got his nickname. But he's most famous for the Wild West shows he produced. Those shows included exciting acts and tales of thrilling escapes, and when Cody wrote the story of his life, he talked about many of the tales as though they'd actually happened. But in reality, he exaggerated the facts and "borrowed" most of the adventures from other cowboys he met. The one story he never exaggerated, though, was how he left his sickbed and rode more than 15 miles to save his dad.

* * *

Real Headline: MAN GLUED TO TOILET SEAT STICKS TO STORY.

Great men never feel great. Small men never feel small. —Chinese proverb

COPYCATS

Being a copycat in school can get you into loads of trouble. But for many animals, insects, and plants, copying is a great way to survive.

YOU STINK!

The corpse flower—which can grow to be taller than most humans—gives off a smell that mimics the stench of a dead, rotting animal. That may seem gross to us, but it's inviting to flies, carrion beetles, and other insects that feed on dead animals. And corpse flowers use these insects to reproduce. When an insect lands on a corpse flower, its pollen sticks to the bug's legs. As the insect goes from flower to flower, it drops bits of pollen into each new plant, which allows the flowers to make seeds and grow new stinky plants.

EIGHT-LEGGED COWBOY COPYCAT

The bolas spider makes use of a scent copycat trick, too. Its favorite nighttime snack is a male moth. So how does a spider catch a flying bug in the dark? Female moths use special scents called pheromones to attract their mates. The bola spider can produce chemicals that mimic the scent of the moth's pheromones. When male moths pick up the scent, they fly toward the spider. But instead of finding a lady friend, they are greeted by a hungry spider with a secret weapon: the bolas spider holds a short thread of silk with a sticky blob on the end. When the moth gets close, the spider swings the sticky thread like a lasso, catches the moth, and reels it in for lunch.

COPYCAT-ERPILLAR

No animal would want to eat a nasty splat of bird poop, right? That's exactly what the swallowtail butterfly caterpillar counts on. This caterpillar has gray-brown skin with white and black spots, and from a distance, it looks like an unappetizing pile of dry bird droppings. During the day, the caterpillar rests and barely moves at all, so most predators simply mistake it for a pile of poop...and pass it by.

COSTUMED COPYCAT

Another animal that uses poop to its advantage is the Borneo crab spider, which creates a bird-dropping cos-tume to *attract* butterflies. First, it spins a few strands of white silk around its black body. Then it tucks in its legs so it looks like a white-and-black blob. Then it lies in wait. When a butterfly lands nearby to sip some salt and minerals from what looks like fresh bird droppings, the crab spider grabs the butterfly with its front legs and makes a meal of it.

Step aside, Mickey: Walt Disney's first cartoon character was Oswald the Lucky Rabbit.

SCIENCE GOOFS

*Throughout history, so-called scientists proposed
a lot of theories that just weren't true.*

A PUMPING...LIVER?

Today, everyone knows that the heart pumps blood
throughout the body. But in ancient Greece, doctors
believed the liver was actually the center of the circu-
latory system. Most historians give Englishman
William Harvey credit for being the first to correctly
explain how blood circulated in the body; he wrote
about it in 1628. But Arab physician Ibn al-Nafis performed many dissections on human and animal bodies,
and actually identified the process in the 13th century.

IN A FIT OF SELF-ABSORPTION

The ancient Egyptian astronomer
Ptolemy said that Earth was the center
of the universe and everything revolved
around it. He was wrong, of course,
but for more than 1,000 years people
believed him. Finally, in the 1500s,
Polish scientist Nicolaus Copernicus had
a completely different view: the Sun was
actually at the center and Earth revolved
around it. (Copernicus probably wasn't the first
to say this, but he was the first to widely publish
his findings.) Then, in the early 1600s, Italy's

Galileo Galilei invented the telescope and proved Copernicus's theory. It took about 100 years, but eventually, the Sun-centered theory caught on.

HAVE LEAD, NEED GOLD...HMMM?

During the 12th century, men studying the field of alchemy had some interesting ideas. Many of them were looking for the "elixir of life," a substance with magical properties that could make a person live forever. (They never found it.) They also believed that, by using a series of chemical reactions, they could turn lead into gold. (They had no success with that, either.) Today, scientists know that you can't turn one substance into another that has completely different chemical properties.

PLEASE PASS THE DIRTY SCALPEL

It wasn't until the 1860s, when French biologist Louis Pasteur proved that germs caused diseases, that hospitals even considered sterilizing their surgical instruments. Before that, doctors believed that infections just sprang up spontaneously. It didn't occur to them that using unwashed scalpels on multiple patients might be part of the problem.

* * *

Thumper: Your heart pumps about 2,000 gallons of blood every day...and 48 million gallons in a lifetime.

Ouch! Leeches have three sets of jaws and 60 to 100 teeth.

DON'T SPIT OUT THAT GUM!

It's might actually be good for you.

IT'S GOOD FOR YOUR BRAIN

In 2007, researchers at England's University of Northumbria conducted a study on the effects that chewing gum has on memory. Seventy-five people were given a memory test, and 25 of the participants were also given gum to chew. The findings: on average, the gum-chewers had 35 percent higher scores. The scientists think it's because the activity of chewing gum slightly raises the heart rate, which increases blood flow to the brain.

IT'S GOOD FOR YOUR EYES

Chopping onions makes you cry because cutting into the vegetable releases enzymes into the air. Those enzymes dissolve in the water of your eyes, converting the enzymes into sulfuric acid—a painful substance that makes your eyes water. Some professional chefs chew gum to avoid the pain. The chewing makes you breathe through your mouth, which in turn makes you breathe in more of the fumes, keeping them out of your eyes.

IT'S GOOD FOR YOUR TEETH
Forget what grown-ups have told you: your teeth actually benefit from chewing gum...as long as it's sugarless. Chewing gum makes your mouth produce saliva, which cleans your teeth.

IT'S GOOD FOR YOUR EARS
As a plane becomes airborne, the pressure inside it drops. Why? Air pressure is lower at higher elevations. But going from one level of pressure to another can make people sick. So planes that fly higher than 3,000 feet use air-pressurization systems inside their cabins. Sometimes, though, those fancy systems don't get the air pressure quite high enough. The result: some passengers get painfully blocked-up ears. The best way to relieve this is to gently force air out of your ears. And the best way to do that is to chew gum. The motion moves your ears and pushes the air out. Ah, relief!

BEAR HAVEN

We'll admit it, some teachers are cool, and here's one we especially like. Every summer, he welcomes a few unusual guests into his home—wild bears.

MOUNTAIN MAN
For most of his life, Charlie Vandergaw was a high-school science teacher in Anchorage, Alaska. But in the mid-1980s, he retired and bought 40 acres of land in the Alaskan wilderness. There, he set up a homestead called Bear Haven, with just a small main house and a couple of outbuildings. He has no phone, no Internet, and no TV. To reach his property, he has to fly there in a small plane because the closest road is more than 20 miles away. But Vandergaw's not starving for company. He's made some unusual friends— the black and grizzly bears who live nearby.

THE FIRST: BIG JACK

Vandergaw didn't always love bears; at one time, he hunted them. But one summer day in the 1980s, he met a bear whom Vandergaw says "wanted me for a friend." The black bear crawled across the yard on his belly, so Vandergaw did the same. Eventually, they got close enough to touch noses, and Vandergaw named the bear Big Jack. He started feeding Big Jack when he came by.

Soon, other bears began showing up on Vandergaw's property—more than 10 in all. There's Walt, a 500-

pound black bear who ambles through the front door most mornings to say hello. Annie and her cub Peanut like to climb trees on the property. And Cookie is an enormous grizzly who loves to play. Vandergaw says, "She'd come in and just play with the irrigation system and I'd feed her. She eventually let me feed her out of my hand."

BRING IN THE LAW

Feeding bears by hand, though, is illegal in Alaska. In fact, feeding any wild animal is against the law there. Authorities worry that feeding wild animals makes them feel too comfortable with humans, which also makes them more willing to come into areas where people live.

New Zealand's kiwi bird is about the size of a chicken, but its eggs are 10 times larger.

Bear attacks on humans are rare—only 20 people died from bear attacks in Alaska in the entire 20th century. (Between 1975 and 1985 alone, 19 Alaskans were killed by dogs.) But when bears do attack, they usually kill. In 2003, an environmentalist named Timothy Treadwell, who'd been living among wild bears on and off for 13 years, was mauled and killed in Alaska's wilderness. His story gained national attention because Treadwell had been making a documentary about his experience, and the event scared a lot of people.

So Alaska's government has been trying to close down Bear Haven for years. Thus far, though, Vandergaw hasn't budged. He's heard all the criticisms and agrees that most people (kids especially) should never approach or try to feed one of these animals. His situation is unique, he believes, because he invites the bears to his home, rather than invades their forest territories like Treadwell did. And plus, he isn't scared of his bears. Vandergaw says, "I don't even think about being eaten. Why would they want to eat me?"

* * *

BLUE BEARS?

It's true...sort of. Technically, they're "glacier bears"— black bears with bluish-black coats. The coloring probably evolved during the last Ice Age (about 18,000 years ago) so the bears could blend into their icy blue habitat in southeastern Alaska. Today, only about 100 of the blue bears exist in the world.

THINGS TO DO IF YOU'RE DEAD

Have you ever wondered what happens to bodies that are donated to science?

CADAVER CAPERS

Most people are buried or cremated after they die. But some choose to donate their bodies to science. That means they allow scientists and medical students to study them after they're dead. But Uncle John wanted to know—what exactly happens to the bodies?

MEDICAL SCIENCE

Most bodies donated to science go to medical schools, where students use them to learn medical techniques. Three or four students usually "share" a body. They take turns dissecting it and examining it as part of their medical training. They might practice surgeries or learn how the different internal organs actually look.

Doctors practice on bodies, too. Surgeons who want to learn new techniques use different parts of donated bodies. For example, a doctor who wants to learn how to do a new kind of face-lift would get a severed head to work with. Another doctor who is practicing knee surgery might examine the same corpse's leg.

DOWN ON THE FARM

"Body farms" are outdoor labs where human bodies are left outside to decompose. Once a body has broken down, scientists study how different conditions might affect it. For example, hot weather will make a body rot faster than cold weather. Crime investigators can then use that information as a model for finding out how long ago a person died and sometimes even whether or not he was murdered.

Forensic entomology—the study of how insects affect human corpses—is a new kind of science being studied at body farms. Forensic entomologists try to determine how long a person has been dead based on the types of insects that live or feed on the bodies. For example, if earthworms are living under a body, that means it's been undisturbed for at least a week. But if beetles are there, the body hasn't been moved in months.

CRASH-TEST DEAD DUMMIES

Another use for dead bodies: to test automobile safety. Many car manufacturers start out using plastic crash-test dummies—mannequins with built-in equipment to measure the force of an accident. But the joints of crash-test dummies don't move the same way human joints do. It's also hard to tell what kind of injuries a real person might get in a crash by looking at broken plastic. So the car companies also use bodies. Some of the most important advances in car safety—like shoulder seatbelts and air bags—were tested on human bodies.

THE GREAT HOUDINI

David Copperfield? David Blaine? Please! Harry Houdini is history's most famous magician, and he pulled off some incredible tricks that still astound people today.

INVENTING HOUDINI

Harry Houdini wasn't his real name. The kid who grew up to be Houdini was born Ehrich Weiss in Hungary in 1874, and moved to the United States with his family when he was four. They settled first in Appleton, Wisconsin, and then moved to New York City.

Houdini showed promise as an escape artist and performer at a young age. Sometimes, he broke into locked kitchen cabinets to steal treats. And his first appearance onstage came when he was just nine. He called himself "Ehrich, Prince of the Air" and put on a show in which he swung from a trapeze.

As a teenager, he decided to perform in magic shows for money. He admired a French magician named Jean Eugène Robert-Houdin, and friends and family had called Ehrich "Ehrie" when he was a kid. So he put the two together to come up with the stage name Harry Houdini.

GREAT ESCAPES

Harry Houdini performed all over New York City and on Coney Island, the city's seaside amusement park. Sometimes he worked alone; other times, he performed with his brother Theo, and later, Bess Rahner, a singer and dancer he married in 1894.

But his magic shows weren't particularly interesting, and his tricks weren't unique. So in 1895, Harry, Theo, and Bess joined a traveling circus, hoping to gain more experience performing for a wider group of people. That's where Houdini found his true calling as an escape artist.

In their circus act, he and Theo performed a trick where they switched places inside a locked trunk. People loved it, and Houdini spent hours each day trying to improve it. He also experimented with escapes from handcuffs, safes, and other locked objects.

The more escapes he put in his act, the more famous he became. Houdini even ran an ad offering $100 to anyone who gave him a pair of handcuffs he couldn't get out of. (No one ever came up with any.) Finally, in 1900, he put on a show at Scotland Yard, the headquarters of London's police department, where he was chained to a pole but escaped. After that, he became a superstar.

HARRY IN A CAN

Houdini perfected dozens of escapes, but his most

famous usually included locks, handcuffs, and being buried alive or submerged in water. One of his most famous tricks was the "Milk Can Escape." Houdini called it "the greatest escape I've ever invented." It worked like this: A handcuffed Houdini climbed into a milk can. (In the early 1900s, dairy farmers often delivered milk in decorated metal cans that stood two or three feet high.) Then his assistants filled the can with water, locked him inside, and surrounded the can with a screen so that the audience couldn't see how Houdini did the trick. About two minutes later, he appeared from behind the screen, dripping wet and gasping for breath...and the audience cheered.

Many people thought Houdini must have had supernatural powers to be able to perform the tricks he did. But the truth was just that he practiced constantly and was incredibly skilled with locks. In the case of the "Milk Can Escape," he only had to break the seal of the lid, wiggle his way out of the can, and then pick the lock on his handcuffs.

JUST SAY BOO

Houdini's other passion was debunking ghost stories. In the early 20th century, a group of people called Spiritualists said they could talk to the dead by holding special ceremonies called séances. People paid huge amounts of money to come to the séances, hoping to speak with their deceased loved ones. Sometimes the loved ones even appeared as ghostly apparitions...or so people thought.

Houdini didn't buy it. He was so skilled with trickery that he believed the ghosts who showed up had to be illusions. So he attended séances all over the United States, revealed the tricks, and exposed the hosts as frauds.

CURTAIN CALL

One of Houdini's stage tricks was to allow someone to punch him hard in the stomach while he remained standing and didn't flinch or show any pain. How did he do it? By doing vigorous exercises ahead of time to strengthen his stomach muscles, and then tightening them before the blow to protect his internal organs. One day in 1926, a fan asked if he could try it out. Houdini agreed, but the fan hit him before Houdini was ready. The blow ruptured his appendix, and he died a few days later.

It wasn't the end of Houdini, however. Spiritualists tried to contact his ghost. (He never answered.) And hundreds of magicians and escape artists who came after him—including David Copperfield and David Blaine—list Houdini as an inspiration.

Want to learn how to do your own magic tricks? Grab your white rabbit and materialize on page 145.

Popular fast-food snack in Japan: *Takoyaki,* or octopus dumplings.

SCAREDY-CAT

Everyone has phobias, even Uncle John. (He's got "dirtythroneophobia.") Here's a list of some phobias he finds funny—plus a few that make him cower in fear.

Ablutophobia: fear of washing or bathing

Selenophobia: fear of the moon

Ecclesiophobia: fear of church

Dentophobia: fear of the dentist

Genuphobia: fear of knees

Geniophobia: fear of chins

Lachanophobia: fear of vegetables

Hippopotomonstrosesquippedaliophobia: fear of long words

Hodophobia: fear of traveling on roads

Octophobia: fear of the figure 8

Triskaidekaphobia: fear of the number 13

Paraskavedekatriaphobia: fear of Friday the 13th

Scolionophobia: fear of school

Philemaphobia: fear of kissing

Panophobia: fear of everything

Phobophobia: fear of phobias

CODE TALKERS

*What's the best way to send messages during
wartime? Hire a special group of Americans
to create an unbreakable code.*

FEELING INSECURE

During World War II, the U.S. Army and Navy
were having a terrible time sending messages
within their ranks. The Japanese had found ways to
intercept and break every code the Americans came up
with. Not wanting to have that same trouble, the
Marines needed a code the Japanese couldn't crack. A
man named Philip Johnston provided the solution.

LANGUAGE OF THE FEW

In 1942, Johnston was living in California and working
as an engineer. But as a child, he'd spent most of his
time on Navajo Indian reservations all over the United
States. His father was a Protestant missionary who
brought the family along while he did his work, and as a
child, Johnston had played with Navajo children and
learned to speak their language.

Now in his 50s, he heard that the U.S. Marines were
looking for a way to send secret messages to each other,
and he immediately thought of his childhood friends.
The Navajo language seemed perfect: it was only spo-
ken—there were no written words—and very few people in the world could understand it.

WHALES AND HUMMINGBIRDS

Johnston took his idea to Major James E. Jones, who was stationed at a Marine base in Oceanside, California. Jones thought the idea was interesting, but he wasn't sure it would work because there weren't any Navajo words for military terms. They couldn't just use English words for things like "tank"—that would make the code easy to crack.

But Johnston had a solution. Instead of using English words, he suggested they assign Navajo words to stand in for the military terms the language lacked. For example, they could use the Navajo word for "whale" to mean "battleship," and the word for "hummingbird" could mean "fighter plane."

Jones was impressed, and he asked Johnston to demonstrate the code for his commanding officers. Everything went so well that, in the spring of 1942, the Marines were allowed to hire and train 29 Navajos for the job. They became known as "code talkers."

READY FOR BATTLE

Those first 29 men helped to create the code. They decided which words would mean what, and then memorized the list...about 450 words. But what if they needed a new word, one that wasn't on the list? They had a solution for that, too. In those cases, the message sender would transmit what sounded like a mixed-up collection of Navajo words. But the message receiver would know to translate the Navajo words into English. Then, the first letter of each English word would spell out the word being sent. For example, a message might look like this:

tsah = <u>N</u>eedle
wol-la-chee = <u>A</u>nt
ah-keh-di-glini = <u>V</u>ictor
tsah-ah-dzoh = <u>Y</u>ucca

And the word would be "Navy."

READY FOR ACTION

The first 29 Navajo code talkers headed off to war in 1942 and were stationed all over the Pacific. By 1945, more than 350 Navajos had joined the Marines as code talkers. They played a role in almost every major American victory over the Japanese, especially the crucial 1945 Battle of Iwo Jima. According to one of the soldiers, "Were it not for the Navajos, the Marines would never have taken Iwo Jima."

The Japanese managed to intercept many of the Navajo messages, but they were never able to crack them. Finally, in August 1945, thanks in part to the Navajo soldiers, the Americans and their allies won World War II.

The white rhino and black rhino are both the same color: Gray.

MORE BIZARRE ANIMAL ACTS

In the wild world of animals, some are wilder than others.
(The first part of the story appears on page 7.)

POLLY WANNA ROLLER-SKATE?
Kiri, a Congo African gray parrot from Seattle, Washington, is a star roller skater. She wears small skates that her trainer, Tani Robar, taught her to use, and shows off her roller disco moves...for peanuts. During her shows, as applause eggs her on, Kiri pushes each leg forward until she reaches the end of the stage. Then the parrot turns, skates back to center stage, and twirls in a circle.

Kiri does other tricks, too. She loads groceries into a mini shopping cart and pushes it wherever Robar says. She also rolls a bowling ball down a ramp into a set of pins. And she plays dead. Kiri lies very still on her back while holding daisies—so she's "pushing up daisies."

STOP, THIEF!

Coatimundis are Central American mammals that look like raccoons with long noses. They are intelligent, inquisitive, and often destructive. In Costa Rica, coatimundis are known for stealing tourists' lunches and backpacks.

But Chicago animal trainer Samantha Martin has one named Callie in her Amazing Animals show. Even though Martin describes coatimundis as "nightmares as pets," Callie is pretty talented. For one trick, she uses her long snout to pickpocket a wallet. Callie also rolls out a red carpet and walks it just like a celebrity.

NOW THAT'S SPEC-CAT-ULAR

Samantha Martin also trains cats. In her Acro-Cats show, felines walk on a high wire, skateboard, and jump through hoops. But most impressive is the all-cat band called the Rock Cats that plays working (but small) guitars, keyboards, and drums. Martin recognizes the band's appeal, but critiques them honestly: "The drummer has no rhythm. The guitar player is always off pitch. The piano player is in her own world."

* * *

REAL FLUBBED HEADLINES

INCLUDE YOUR CHILDREN WHEN BAKING COOKIES

KIDS MAKE NUTRITIOUS SNACKS

HIGH SCHOOL DROPOUTS CUT IN HALF

MAN FOUND DEAD IN CEMETERY

HOSPITALS SUED BY 7 FOOT DOCTORS

WRONG FACTS

*Some more things you may have learned
in school that just aren't true.*

FACT? *Africa's Sahara is the world's largest desert.*
WRONG! When most people think of a desert, they
think of a vast sea of sand with the hot sun beating
down. But the technical definition of a desert is a place
that receives little to no rainfall.

By that measure, the largest desert on earth is
Antarctica. Even though it's cold and is covered almost
entirely with ice, the continent receives nearly no rain,
making it the world's largest desert.

FACT? *The word "ain't" isn't in the dictionary.*
WRONG! It's may be poor grammar to use the word
"ain't," as in "I ain't going to say 'isn't.'" But just
because a word is incorrect doesn't mean it's not in
the dictionary.

Dictionaries aren't necessarily authorities on "right"
and "wrong" words—they're merely catalogs of all the
words in a language. So "ain't" is listed as a
slang word in most English dictionaries.
But that doesn't mean it's okay to use.
(In fact, there are lots of words in the
dictionary that will get you into far
more trouble than "ain't.")

Superstitious President Franklin D. Roosevelt refused to sit at a table set for 13 guests.

BLACKBEARD'S LOOT

*On the final leg of our treasure hunt, we sail north.
The notorious pirate Blackbeard supposedly stowed
his stash off the coast of New England,
but the question is...where?*

SEEKING: Silver ingots, silver Spanish dollars, gold coins, and pouches of gold dust.
LAST SEEN... On the Isles of Shoals, off the coast of New Hampshire and Maine.

LEGEND: For years, Captain Blackbeard (a.k.a. Edward Teach) terrorized travelers along the North American coast. He was intimidating to look at. Standing more than six feet tall, he decorated his long beard and curly black hair with beads and black ribbons. His ship—the *Queen Anne's Revenge*—was just as intimidating. It was manned by menacing pirates, armed with cannons, and protected with reinforced sides. When seafarers saw the *Revenge* coming, they usually didn't bother to fight. They just handed over whatever precious goods they had on board.

England's Royal Navy was charged with the task of trying to catch Blackbeard. And in the early 1700s, the authorities closed in on him near Canada. So he and his crew split up their loot and parted ways. Legend says

Blackbeard headed for the sparsely populated Isles of Shoals, a group of nine islands off the New England coast. There, he anchored the *Revenge*, married a girl he'd brought from Scotland, and they stayed for their honeymoon. Blackbeard staked out a spot for his treasure and hid it while his wife roamed the island.

THE BIG GUNS ARE COMING!

But one day in 1718, a British warship appeared in the distance. In a hurry, Blackbeard either ditched his new bride or asked her to stay behind to guard the loot. Either way, she remained on the islands until she died in 1735. (Some say she's still there, haunting the area and whispering, "He will come again.")

Blackbeard sailed for the Carolinas, where the Royal Navy eventually caught and killed him. (The soldiers cut off his head and hung it from his ship's bow to scare other would-be thieves.) Just before that final battle, a fellow pirate asked Blackbeard if his wife knew where the treasure was. The captain replied that nobody but he and the devil knew where it was, and that "the longest liver shall take it."

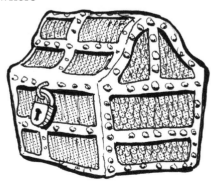

UNDISCOVERED RICHES

It's hard to know just how much treasure

Blackbeard collected over the years, but some of the ships he plundered kept records. We know he snatched a fortune—including 400,000 silver Spanish dollars—from two ships in 1717. He also stole loot from his own crew that's worth over $300,000 today. Like most pirates, Blackbeard spent his money recklessly, but he also claimed to have hidden some.

KEEP LOOKING

People have been searching the Isles of Shoals for Blackbeard's treasure for centuries. Someone did find a few silver ingots under a rock on one of the islands (called Smuttynose) in the 1800s, but no one knows for sure if the pieces were Blackbeard's.

Most treasure hunters believe that if the fortune is there, it's probably buried on Smuttynose, Appledore, Star, or Lunging Island. Why? Blackbeard could have easily sailed to any of them, and there are lots of good hiding spots. Lunging is shaped like a dumbbell, and at high tide, the ocean rises over the center, marking a clear spot where someone could bury his loot when the water recedes. There also used to be a cave nearby—it's underground now. In the 1950s, sonar tests showed that the cave might contain metal—perhaps silver. But no one's been able to get to it. And in 2000, the History Channel even sent geologists to search Lunging Island. But no treasure has been discovered...yet.

Swim over to the first two treasure tales on pages 50 and 97.

Book actually published in 1981: *The Pictorial Book of Tongue Coating.*

THE BIGGEST

Did you know that Porter the Wonder Dog has the biggest appetite at the Bathroom Readers' Institute? He can eat 10 dog treats in one sitting! (The rest of us can't even eat one.) Here are some other "biggest" things.

...SWIMMING POOL

The San Alfonso del Mar resort in Chile is home to the largest swimming pool in the world. It's more than half a mile long (3,323 feet), holds 66 million gallons of water, and is 115 feet deep at its deepest point. The water is always a comfy 79°F, and it's not just for swimming: you can scuba dive, kayak, snorkel, and sail on it.

...POOL TOY

If you're going to play in that pool, you'll need an enormous pool toy. Consider this one: in 2001, a company in Ontario, Canada, built a "pool noodle" that was a mile long...even longer than the pool in Chile!

...OBJECT REMOVED FROM A HUMAN SKULL

In 1998, an intruder at a friend's house in Jacksonville, Florida, stabbed Michael Hill in the head with an eight-inch hunting knife. Hill didn't feel any pain at first and even walked to another house with the knife still in his brain. A friend rushed him to the hospital, where doctors carefully removed the knife. Within a week, Hill was well enough to go home.

...TOWER OF BOWLING BALLS

In 1998, David Kremer from Wisconsin stacked 10 bowling balls on top of each other. Here's the really amazing part—he didn't use any glue. The balls were perfectly balanced.

...GOLDFISH

In 2002, an aquarium in Hong Kong, China, found itself the owner of the world's largest goldfish. Called Bruce, he was more than 15 inches long...about the size of an average cat.

There are three types of people—those who can count and those who can't.

DROPOUTS CAN SUCCEED

The next time you're struggling with homework, think about this: some of the most successful people in history dropped out—or were kicked out—of school.

THE NUTTY PROFESSOR

Albert Einstein dropped out of high school when he was 16 because he felt that the school he was attending in Germany was too strict. Even earlier, some teachers had suggested that he quit grade school. Albert had a speech impediment, so his parents and teachers worried he might be "backward." Later, of course, he went on to college, became a world-famous physicist and lecturer, and was even offered the job of president of Israel. (He declined.)

OFF TO SEE THE WIZARD

Thomas Edison was kicked out of school at the age of seven—just three months after he enrolled. His teacher called him unruly and slow, so his parents homeschooled him. But he went on to invent the phonograph, perfect the lightbulb, and receive 1,093 U.S. patents, making him one of the most prolific inventors in history. Edison invented so many things that a newspaper reporter nicknamed him the "Wizard of Menlo Park" (the New Jersey town where he lived).

IT'S BURGERS FOR YOU!

When he was 15, Dave Thomas had a job as a restaurant busboy in Fort Wayne, Indiana. His parents were moving, but he wanted to stay in Fort Wayne, so Thomas quit school and moved in with the restaurant's owners. He later moved on to executive-level jobs at Kentucky Fried Chicken and became a millionaire at the age of 35. Then he founded the fast-food restaurant Wendy's. Dave Thomas finally got his GED (a high school diploma) when he was 61 years old. But he spent almost his entire working life in the fast-food industry...though he hired other people—about 40,000 of them—to do the actual burger flipping.

THE TECHIE DROPOUT CLUB

Bill Gates dropped out of Harvard University in 1975. He'd been a pre-law student, but actually spent most of his time fiddling with the machines in the school's computer center. He finally left school because a childhood friend (and fellow college dropout) named Paul Allen convinced him to try his hand at running a little computer company that they called Microsoft.

Another tech millionaire also left school in 1975: Steve Wozniak dropped out of the University of California at Berkeley and went on to found the computer company Apple Inc. with Steve Jobs (who had dropped out of Oregon's Reed College). Wozniak eventually went back to Berkeley. Using the pseudonym "Rocky Raccoon Clark," he got an electrical engineering/computer science degree in 1986.

YUK, YUK, YUK

See if you can stump your teacher with these jokes.

Q. What did the lips say to the eyes?
A. Between you and me, something smells.

Q. Where does January come after February?
A. In the dictionary.

Q. Why was the skeleton afraid to cross the road?
A. He had no guts.

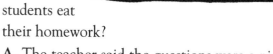

Q. Why did all the students eat their homework?
A. The teacher said the questions were a piece of cake.

Q. Who invented airplanes that didn't fly?
A. The Wrong brothers.

Q. Why was the computer so chilly?
A. He forgot to close his Windows.

...A: Like Mensa, they're societies for people with super-high IQ scores.

15 WAYS TO GET DETENTION

Can you find all the forbidden things that we've hidden in the grid to the right? (Remember, when you report to detention, leave the whoopee cushion at home.)

BAD LANGUAGE

BEING RUDE

BURPING REALLY LOUD

EATING IN CLASS

FARTING FREQUENTLY

KICKING

LAUNCHING SPITBALLS

PINCHING

PULLING PIGTAILS

SNORING IN CLASS

SPITTING

STEALING LUNCHES

TALKING ON CELL

TELLING FIBS

THROWING NOTEBOOK

The granite of Mount Rushmore erodes at the rate of one inch every 10,000 years.

```
L F B B S A C S Z T W T E H
X A D M E P I N C H I N G L
A R U E H U O O X R C T A A
G T O I C L D R Z O X D U U
M I L L N L P I P W B X G N
G N Y Q U I W N W I E E N C
Q G L H L N Q G B N T R A H
O F L S G G F I S G A T L I
C R A R N P T N V N L E D N
R E E F I I D C P O K L A G
G Q R X L G X L C T I L B S
P U G Q A T V A C E N I X P
P E N G E A F S J B G N A I
G N I T T I P S A O O G F T
M T P F S L C V X O N F H B
J L R H M S G N I K C I K A
O Y U E D U R G N I E B J L
D X B L M P D Z F C L S T L
K E A T I N G I N C L A S S
```

Answers on page 243.

DOES MONEY GROW ON TREES?

Adults are always saying, "Money doesn't grow on trees, you know!" But that's not actually true...about paper money, anyway. Here's the history of the kind of money that <u>does</u> come from trees.

THAT'LL BE 20 SHELLS

Before there was money, people used the barter system—they just traded goods and services with each other. The first actual money came along around 1000 BC, when people living along the coastlines of the Indian and Pacific oceans started trading small shells called cowries for services and supplies. Eventually, people switched from shells to precious metals: gold, silver, bronze, and copper became the standards by which people judged the value of things.

FLYING MONEY

Meanwhile, the Chinese invented paper sometime around AD 100. About 700 years later, there was a copper shortage, so the Chinese emperor decided to substitute decorated pieces of paper, or banknotes, for coins.

Don't forget to celebrate End of the Middle Ages Day on May 29.

The banknotes represented different amounts of copper and silver and could be exchanged for the precious metals. To make them, the Chinese harvested trees and pressed the wood into pieces of rectangular paper; the larger the rectangle, the more money it was worth. People mostly used the paper money to buy goods from faraway places because messengers could carry the paper more easily than bags of coins, and could "fly" (or at least ride horses really fast) across the countryside with the paper notes. So the Chinese called the paper banknotes "flying money."

MARCO! POLO!

In the 13th century, the explorer Marco Polo visited China. When he got back to Italy, people had a hard time believing his stories of the Chinese paper money. At that time, Europeans used gold and silver coins. To them, paper didn't have any value. When Marco Polo suggested that Europe should consider paper money, people laughed at him.

Finally, in 1657, a few Europeans changed their minds. That year, Sweden founded a national bank, managed by the government. The bank's director, Johan Palmstruch, started issuing paper money instead of handing out coins. That worked fine for a while, but by 1664, people had figured out that Palmstruch was printing more banknotes than there were coins in the bank to cover them. That caused a mass panic: the bank collapsed, and Palmstruch went to jail for the rest of his life.

But paper money had taken hold in Europe. It was lightweight and easy to produce. And people who had once carried around heavy coins could now fold up pieces of paper in their pockets instead.

COMING TO AMERICA

Banknotes traveled to the New World with the European colonists. In 1690, Massachusetts was the first area to start using paper money, and eventually all of the colonies followed.

But the different colonies used different kinds of money. So in 1781, during the American Revolution, the Continental Congress (which was in charge of the colonies at the time) opened a national bank: the Bank of North America. And in 1791, after the new country had been officially formed, Congress created a single currency for the United States and issued paper banknotes that made it easy to buy and sell goods from state to state.

These days, banknotes are found all over the world. American dollars, euros, Japanese yen—they're all made from some kind of paper, which is usually comes from trees. But today's U.S. dollars are actually made from a mixture of cotton and linen to make them durable and harder to rip...so, technically, they grow on plants.

In Bram Stoker's novel *Dracula*, no one ever mentions Count Dracula's first name.

HOW TO MAKE CHOCOLATE BUGS

Imagine this: It's lunchtime and your teacher has cafeteria duty. You call her over, offer a tasty snack, and pull out...bugs! Well, not really. They're candy. But here's how to make them.

WHAT YOU'LL NEED

- 2 red licorice whips
- 24 caramels
- 1 cup of chocolate chips
- Red Hots
- Wax paper
- Colored candy sprinkles
- Microwave-safe bowl
- Cookie sheet

DIRECTIONS

- Line your cookie sheet with wax paper.
- Place 12 caramels onto the wax paper and press them with your hand so they're shaped like small ovals.

Only two mammals lay eggs: the duck-billed platypus and the spiny echidna.

- Now it's time to cut the licorice whips into 48 small pieces. (We know it's annoying, but be sure to get your parents' permission before you do any cutting or cooking.)

- Press four pieces of licorice into the sides of each caramel to make legs.

- Put a second caramel on top of each "bug" and press it into an oval shape again. To make sure the legs stay put, be sure to seal the edges where the two caramels meet.

- Put the chocolate chips in a microwave-safe bowl and heat in the microwave on high for 1 minute. Stir the chocolate, and then heat on high for another minute.

- Take the bowl out of the microwave, and stir the chocolate until it's smooth.

- Drizzle chocolate over each "bug."

- Now it's time to decorate: use Red Hots for eyes and sprinkles to give the bodies some color.

- Let the "bugs" cool for about half an hour, and then they're ready for school.

* * *

Every little bit helps: During its lifetime, a worker bee will make about one teaspoon of honey.

MORE BAD WORDS

Here are three more words that'll make you sound smart...but saying them might get you into trouble.

BUTTRESS. This word describes a structure (usually made from brick or stone) that's built against an outside wall to strengthen it. It's also a verb meaning "to support someone," which means you can "buttress your buddy's argument." It comes from the Anglo-French word *boteraz*, or "thrusting arch."

PENAL COLONY. A place where prisoners are sent away from society, this comes from the Old French word *péna*, which meant "punishment" and also gave us the word "penalty."

CRAPPER. If you get in trouble for saying this word, consider explaining that you were speaking of Thomas Crapper, the 19th-century English plumber (and one of Uncle John's heroes) who perfected the modern flush toilet. All of his commodes had "T. Crapper" printed on them, and World War I soldiers popularized his last name as a slang word.

WE'VE GOT RIGHTS

Adults make the rules, but they're not always fair...or reasonable, or even legal. Here are some kids who refused to let anyone trample on their rights.

BUT IT ROTS YOUR TEETH!
In 2008, Michael Sheridan, vice president of his eighth-grade class in Connecticut, got caught buying a bag of Skittles from a classmate...and both of them were suspended for it. Their school had a "no candy sales" policy that was created to help students eat more nutritious food. The policy banned candy and bake sales as fund-raisers, and made sure that only healthy snacks were sold in the school's vending machines. It never occurred to Michael that the rule would also apply to one kid selling a bag of candy to another.

Not only was Michael suspended for three days, he was forced to give up his position as class VP and he was not allowed to attend the school's honor society dinner even though he was a honor student. Michael's mom thought that seemed too harsh for a kid who had never even gotten detention before, so she took his story to the local paper. Soon, Michael discovered that a lot of people felt the same way. Eventually, the school gave in. First, the suspension was reduced from three days to one. Later, Michael was reinstated as class vice president, and his school record was cleared.

PINK HAIR TODAY, SUSPENDED TOMORROW

The color pink symbolizes cancer prevention; at least that's how Amelia Robbins of Mountain Grove, Missouri, saw it. In 2008, the seventh-grader dyed her hair pink as a tribute to her dad, who died of cancer when she was six. Unfortunately, Amelia's school didn't approve: administrators claimed her pink hair distracted other students, and they suspended her.

Miss Crump is a grump

After the school made its decision, Amelia and her mother and stepfather contacted the American Civil Liberties Union (ACLU), a group that helps people fight rules and laws that violate their constitutional rights. The ACLU wrote a letter to the school district on Amelia's behalf. It compared her situation to one from the 1960s in which students in Iowa were suspended for wearing black armbands to protest the Vietnam War. In that case, the U.S. Supreme Court determined that the suspension was unfair because it infringed on the students' constitutional right to free speech.

The court ruled that the armbands were a silent, unobtrusive, but significant way to protest a specific cause. The ACLU claimed the same thing about Amelia's pink hair. They requested that the school let her back in—pink hair and all—clear her record, and let her make up the work she missed without a penalty. Eventually, that's just what the school administrators did.

THE SHOW MUST (NOT) GO ON

One Boulder, Montana, mother protested when her son's high school decided to perform *Grease* as its 2007 end-of-year musical. She objected to the smoking and foul language in the play, and she asked why the show's characters weren't held to the same standards the students had to meet in real life.

The mother's objection caused a big stir (especially after she admitted she'd never seen the play), but the most important question was whether she had the right to prevent audiences from seeing it just because she objected. In the end, the students performed the play, although the drama teacher did cut out some four-letter words and eliminate most of the smoking (the students were using fake cigarettes anyway). But the student body president, who played tough girl Rizzo, summed it up best when she said, "The behaviors in the play don't affect the students. We're not actually doing this. That's why it's called *acting*."

DUMB CROOKS

So you think crime pays? Think again.

TANKS FOR NOTHING

Oops: In November 2008, Fausto Pinos—a landlord in Spring Valley, New York—took the toilet, bathtub, sink, and countertop out of the bathroom of one of his apartments. Why? He was trying to evict a woman who hadn't paid her rent, and figured not having a bathroom would convince her to move. The problem: Renting an apartment without a bathroom is illegal.

Gotcha! The New York Board of Health fined him $10,000.

HE NEEDED SOME Z'S

Oops: In 2008, a burglar broke into a house in Kalamazoo, Michigan. He grabbed a bunch of electronics equipment and then, for some reason, went back inside to take a nap. When the owner came home and found a strange man sleeping on her sofa, she called the police.

Gotcha! The cops woke the burglar and arrested him.

TOUGH GETAWAY

Oops: In 2006, a 20-year-old man (whose name was not released) walked into a convenience store and slipped a package of Pop-Tarts into his pants. When the store clerk confronted him, he hit her in the stomach and ran out of the store.

When the police arrived, they had no trouble finding the pastry thief. Why? He sprinted into the street, tried to dodge traffic, but was eventually hit...by two cars. That slowed him down enough for the police to catch up.

Gotcha! The cops offered medical treatment, but the thief refused, so they took him right to jail.

HOT OFF THE LOT

Oops: Marcus George of Arkansas was paroled from prison in June 2008 after serving a sentence for robbery. A few days later, he and friend stopped by an automobile dealership to test-drive a new car...and never brought it back. A few days later, when George arrived to meet with his parole officer in the stolen car, the police arrested him.

Gotcha! George's parole was revoked and he was sent back to prison.

* * *

FAT CHANCE

Camel humps store fat, which the animals use for energy when they can't find food. The fat usually lasts about two weeks, and if a camel uses it all, the hump will go limp, though eventually it'll grow back to its original size...which can weigh up to 80 pounds.

ANSWERS

WHO AM I, PAGE 24

1. Stich, *Lilo and Stitch*; **2.** SpongeBob, *SpongeBob SquarePants*; **3.** Elroy Jetson, *The Jetsons*; **4.** Timmy Turner, *Fairly Odd Parents*; **5.** Po, *Kung Fu Panda*; **6.** Phineas Flynn and Ferb Fletcher, *Phineas and Ferb*; **7.** Lisa, *The Simpsons*; **8.** Tommy Pickles, *Rugrats*

TOON-EMIES, PAGE 54

1. l **2.** c **3.** d **4.** q **5.** a **6.** e **7.** f **8.** g **9.** o **10.** p **11.** j **12.** n **13.** i **14.** b **15.** r **16.** h

THE CASE OF THE KIDNAPPED KID, PAGE 61

Waldo's story had a hole. He told the inspector that he'd only seen his attacker from the back. But if that were true, he couldn't have known the sweatshirt had a zipper in the front. Waldo finally confessed that he and Winslow had set the whole thing up to get some money from their dad. (The boys wanted to buy dirt bikes and join an extreme-sports circus.)

BRAINTEASERS, PAGE 105

1. One in a million **2.** A pair of pants **3.** Hillbilly **4.** Crossroads **5.** No U Turn **6.** Death Valley

7. Shut up 8. H_2O (water) 9. Cornerstone
10. Railroad crossing 11. Touchdown 12. Double
vision 13. Space Invaders 14. Thundercloud
15. One step forward, two steps back

POP QUIZ, PAGE 160

By serving mashed potatoes.

DRIVE YOUR TEACHER NUTS, PAGE 20

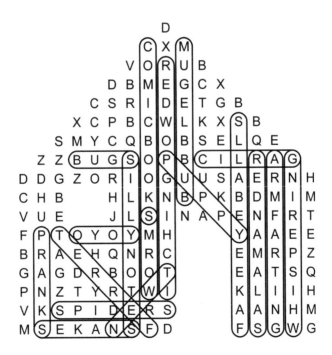

THE CASE OF THE GOOEY SPITBALL, PAGE 138

Mr. Patterson realized that Melissa had been paying attention to the punctuation lesson, and he knew how to interpret her note. It meant: "Question Mark—I saw him throw it!" Mark later confessed to tossing the spitball.

FIFTEEN WAYS TO GET DETENTION, PAGE 228

```
L F B B S A C S Z T W T E H
X A D M E P I N C H I N G L
A R U E H U O O X R C T A A
G T O I C L D R Z O X D U U
M I L L N L P I P W B X G N
G N Y Q U I W N W I E E N C
Q G L H L N Q G B N T R A H
O F L S G G F I S G A T L I
C R A R N P T N V N L E D N
R E E F I I D C P O K L A G
G Q R X L G X L C T I L B S
P U G Q A T V A C E N I X P
P E N G E A F S J B G N A I
G N I T T I P S A O O G F T
M T P F S L C V X O N F H B
J L R H M S G N I K C I K A
O Y U E D U R G N I E B J L
D X B L M P D Z F C L S T L
K E A T I N G I N C L A S S
```

...but only seven people have ever been hit by one.

THE LAST PAGE

FELLOW BATHROOM READERS:
Bathroom reading should never be taken
loosely—we must sit firmly for what we believe
in, even while the rest of the world is taking pot shots
at us.

So Sit Down and Be Counted! Join the Bathroom
Readers' Institute. It's free! Send a self-addressed,
stamped envelope and your e-mail address to:

Bathroom Readers' Institute
P.O. Box 1117
Ashland, OR 97520

You'll receive a free membership card, our BRI newsletter (via e-mail), and exclusive announcements about
special sales, and you'll earn a permanent spot on the
BRI honor roll!

Well, we're out of space, and when you've got to go,
you've got to go. Hope to hear from
you soon, and meanwhile,
remember...

Go with the Flow!